AUTHOR PRENEUR

*How to Build an Empire
and Become the AUTHORity
in Your Business*

SHANDA TROFE

AUTHORPRENEUR

How to Build an Empire and Become the Authority in Your Business

ISBN-13: 978-1-7374553-9-4

First Edition June 2016
Second Edition February 2022

Transcendent Publishing
PO Box 66202
St. Pete Beach, FL 33736
www.TranscendentPublishing.com

Printed in the United States of America.

TRANSCENDENT
publishing

For my students and clients—my tribe—without whom I'd have no purpose, and this work would be pointless. I wrote this book for you.

Contents

Sunny Dawn Johnston

As an Authorpreneur, I have been blessed to spread my message through the written word over the past twenty-two years. I have traveled the world speaking to sold-out audiences in the thousands, written over twenty books and workbooks, developed multiple online courses and membership programs, and created dozens of products to support the message I share in my books and courses. Ultimately, I have created a successful business doing what I LOVE to do. I truly am an Authorpreneur, even though I didn't know what one was.

When Shanda Trofe approached me asking if I would be willing to write the foreword for her book, *Authorpreneur,* I first asked her to explain what an Authorpreneur was. Once I heard the definition, I immediately said yes. It felt like a perfect fit. Not only did I want to support Shanda's book, but I wanted to support Shanda. From the day I met her at my healing retreat in Sedona, Arizona back in 2012, I knew she was destined for success. I saw her as a dedicated, driven and downright inspiring woman. I knew she was an amazing writer; I could feel it. As we sat in the kitchen early one morning, she shared with me some of her fears of "getting out there" in the world with her writing. Those fears you can probably relate to as well; I know I did. The thing with Shanda was she pushed through them. She didn't let those fears scare her away from her dream, but instead they motivated her into action as she stepped into each and every one of them. Within a few months, she had written her first book. I did say she was a go-getter, right?

So, here we are several years later and not only is Shanda an excellent writer and author, but her passion has naturally progressed into publishing and teaching … … and lucky for you it did. She is a voracious student, taking class after class on how to create success, and now, by sharing the knowledge in this book, she is offering you the keys to success as well.

That is why I am so excited about the possibilities she is creating for YOU, the reader, by offering this book. The contents of this book are LIFE CHANGING and should not be taken lightly. This book you hold in your hands offers you the tools to create your business into one of intention, focus and success. All you have to do is:

- **Begin** – You must start somewhere and *Authorpreneur* tells you exactly how to start in simple, clear and easy-to-understand steps.

- **Build** – There are many roads to success and they take tons of time, energy and money. *Authorpreneur* takes the guesswork out and offers you many tried and true methods.

- **Believe** – When you have a message within you and the roadmap to follow a step-by-step plan, you know that success can be yours … if you will believe in yourself and implement, implement, implement these tools and techniques Shanda offers.

As an aspiring writer, I didn't know where to start. I didn't know how to outline my book, which kept me from writing it for years. I had an idea in my head, but was afraid I would do it wrong, so I just never did it. Maybe you relate? So many of us have a heart's desire to write and share what you have learned in the hopes that it will help someone else. Yet, I didn't know how to do it "right," so I didn't do anything. Man, what I would have given to have *Authorpreneur* at that time. It took me five more years and lots of heartache before I finally realized my dream of becoming a published author.

Throughout my journey as a writer/author/creator, I had to become a student. It wasn't a choice. As a writer, I found myself having to learn how to be an author. It wasn't just about writing a great book anymore, there was a whole list of things I needed to learn. From brand development to platform, list building to promotion, products to publishing ... and so much more in between. It was not only overwhelming but expensive and time consuming. I muddled my way through most of it and had some hard knocks along the learning journey. As an author, I needed to figure out how then to create products to support my message. This was a bit easier for me, but I still had many lessons to learn, ones that this book could have saved me from as well.

Authorpreneur is the book I dreamed of having when I began my career. Oh, how I wished then that someone would just share the secrets of the industry, the do's and don'ts, the have to's and the skips, but there was no such book out there at that time. This is what excited me so about this book.

Authorpreneur has taken out all of the guesswork and offered clearly defined steps to success. Whether you are just beginning or are a seasoned writer, the information in this book will save you hundreds, if not thousands of head-banging hours trying to figure out how to grow your business and your career. You will learn the how to's of the publishing world. It will leave you with peace of mind and confidence in knowing you are completely capable of spreading your message with the world ... a message the world deserves to hear.

In this book, you will receive the step-by-step instructions, anecdotes, and so many tools necessary to walk the journey of an Authorpreneur. Are you ready? You've already taken the first step; you have the book. Now simply turn the page and begin one of the greatest journeys of your life.

~Sunny Dawn Johnston
- Bestselling author of over twenty books,
and creator of *Elev8 Your Life* and *My Spiritual Biz*
www.sunnydawnjohnston.com

Introduction

As business professionals, we often frequent mixers and networking events, collecting and exchanging business cards with the hopes of connecting with those who may benefit from what we have to offer. But whatever happens to all those cards? Do they get stuffed into wallets, behind the AAA card, or stuck to the kids' school photos perhaps? How often do they get tossed aside, or end up in the trash, nonetheless?

What if you had a physical book, in lieu of a business card, to act as a polished product for your business? There's no better representation of you and your brand than a published book that lends instant credibility as an expert in your field, or area of expertise. When it's done right, there's something about becoming a published author and creating a high-quality book to represent your business that opens doors to new opportunity and expansion. What's more, books tend to end up on desks or coffee tables, not tossed in the trash or shoved into wallets. The days of passing out cards are far behind us; in today's day and age there's no reason not to have a published book as a product for your business. And those who do are ahead of the game.

But it's not enough just to write and publish a book, crafting a *quality* book is the key. You won't want to hand out a mediocre version or thrown-together product that screams DIY. Your book is the ultimate extension of you and your brand, and should be treated with the same care and diligence you used to plan and launch your business.

In the pages ahead, I am going to show you exactly how to do just that. As a bestselling author, book coach, and publishing consultant, I aim to educate you on all areas of the publishing industry, while offering inside information on the best tools and resources to help you craft a quality book that will serve as an essential product for your business.

My Story

Back in 2012, I set out to create a product for my own business. Aside from being the CEO of Transcendent Publishing, my passion was (and still is) working with writers, specifically aspiring authors, and I found that I was starting to build a nice reputation for myself by coaching aspiring authors through the book-writing process. But there are many writing coaches out there doing the same, so I had to find a way to set my skills apart from the rest.

As the founder of Spiritual Writers Network, I seemed to be attracting spiritual writers into my circle at the time, many with an important message to share, yet most didn't know how to find the courage to open old wounds and delve deep within to let their story unfold. I found myself working with clients who were experiencing fear about the writing process and who needed a little extra coaching in order to write their book and tell their story authentically. One encouragement I found myself repeating over and over to my clients was to write from the heart. I truly believe, when we get out of our ego-based thinking and allow our creativity to emerge, that's when our most heart-felt writing comes forward. Now, I believe in structure and writing systems that must be set in place to create a quality book, but I found I was also using a variety of spiritual-based techniques to urge them to unlock their creativity. Before long, I knew I had found a niche in the writing industry—I no longer was *just* a writing coach, I was a heart-based writing coach who worked primarily, at the time, with aspiring spiritual authors.

It was August of 2013 when I attended a networking conference for women in business. I was so inspired by all the coaches and speakers at the event that I left with a clear message and plan of action. I knew I needed to brand myself, and create a product specific to my niche. After some brainstorming and planning, I decided to brand myself as the Write from the Heart Writing Coach. But that was just the beginning. Next, I wrote and published a book to act as a product for my business and an extension of my brand. Guess what the book was titled? *Write from the Heart: A Step-by-Step Writing Guide to Get Your Message from Idea to Publication.*

I strategically launched *Write from the Heart* using some of the techniques I'll teach you within this very book. I quickly reached the bestsellers list within the first five days of publication, and that book went on to sell thousands of copies before I removed it from print. But the book was just the tip of the iceberg. From there I saw the potential to turn the concepts I wrote about in my book into an online course, and before long the *Write from the Heart: 8-Week Book Writing Intensive* was born. This became my most popular product and service and it was easy to create since I already had much of the content from my book.

But I didn't stop there. I had my own radio show titled, *Write from the Heart*, where I interviewed a different author each week and discussed topics such as writing and publishing. I created a companion journal to publish as a second product based upon my book, and created a CD of affirmations for writers with a meditation to unlock creativity and expand productivity. I also created an affirmation card deck to sell at events alongside my book, CD, and journal, and I hosted writing retreats and various workshops—all based on the theories of my book.

To make a long story short, my business went from working with writers (a general niche) to narrowing down my area of expertise and finding my ideal avatar, or client, and then creating products to reach them specifically. After I wrote my book, I repurposed the content and created a viable business and products to support that business around my brand. When people heard Write from the Heart, they thought of me, and I had my book, products, and brand to thank for that.

Fast forward to 2022, and I've repeated this process with each book I've published, and I'm getting ready to do it once again with my next book, *Self-Publishing Success: How to Write a Nonfiction Book that Makes an Impact and Publish It Like a Pro*. Now my niche has evolved to working primarily with nonfiction authors who desire to write and self-publish a high-quality book for their business, or create a business based on the message within their book. I've already begun growing the Facebook group, Self-Publishing Success, where I'm establishing myself as the expert and providing value to indie authors. Additionally, for the past three years I've been training authorpreneurs through my flagship program, the Author Success Academy, where I teach my students how to write a bestselling book, build their author platform, and publish and launch their transformational book to the world … the right way.

That is what I am going to share with you in the pages ahead. I'm going to show you how to find your niche, develop a brand, write and publish a high-quality book as the foundation of your business, with ways to build your platform and create companion products and services based on that book and your brand. You'll learn how to craft an all-around lucrative business model that will ensure you are not just an entrepreneur, nor just an author. I'm going to show you how to build your brand and create quality products that will help you become the authority in your business by becoming an *authorpreneur.*

Are you ready to build your empire?

Good. You've come to the right place.

How to Use this Book

Throughout this book, I offer a variety of tools and techniques you can incorporate to build your list, create products and services for your business, and grow your empire. While everything I mention may not be for you, pick and choose that which resonates with you, and then make a concerted effort to learn more on how to implement them to effectively grow your business.

I believe in a lean startup, so if you are just getting started building your business you won't want to do it all at once—Rome wasn't built in a day, after all. But you will want to continue to reinvest in your business. Each time you achieve success on one product, take a portion of the profits and invest in a new product, service or program for your empire.

While I couldn't possibly break down every technique and exactly how to implement it in this book (a single book could be written on each topic), I will give you an overview of how each works along with valuable resources to find more information, and then you can decide if you want to explore it further. I promise to offer as much information as I can in the space allotted so that you can get a feel for all your options. And if you decide you want to delve further, visit me over at www.shandatrofe.com where you will find a free list of **My Top 20 Tools for Building an Author Empire.** These are the tools, software and programs I used to build my own empire, and I will gladly share them all with you.

To your success,
Shanda Trofe

CHAPTER ONE

What is an Authorpreneur?

The definition of an authorpreneur varies, depending on who you ask. Some say an authorpreneur is someone who builds a business around writing books. Do I agree? Yes and no. I do believe you can build a decent income writing books alone; in fact, we'll even discuss the tools for creating a series of books later. It can be done, I know many successful authors making a good monthly income publishing eBooks alone, for example, many of them my clients. But I want to encourage you to look above and beyond just writing a book, or books, if you will.

For me, an authorpreneur is someone who builds a lucrative empire using a variety of products that strategically funnel into one another and progressively build upon each other. An authorpreneur will have a published book as a product for his business, yes, but he won't stop there. An authorpreneur will think outside the box and see the bigger picture.

One of my mentors once asked me if I consider myself an author or a writer. "That's easy," I told her. "I'm published, so that makes me an author."

"Not exactly."

"Really? How so?"

"A writer is someone who enjoys the act of writing, often in solitude, and often is introverted by nature, as many writers are," she explained. "An author is someone who enjoys everything that comes along with being published. The marketing, the networking, the speaking engagements, being in the public eye, self-promotion. You can be published, but if you don't like the marketing and self-promotional side of the business, then you are more of a writer than an author."

At the time her response shook me. But she was right. To me, she epitomized everything that an author should be. She had just returned from traveling the country for a year on a self-funded book tour to share her message. She was often booked for speaking engagements where she would share her message and then do book signings and workshops where she sold her books and other products. She was well-known on social media and YouTube, and had a huge mailing list for her email marketing. At the time, that seemed unattainable for me, and quite frankly seemed like it would take a lot of time, energy and money to build, so I had to decide if it was right for me.

The more I thought about it, I realized that I enjoyed the act of writing and creating more than I enjoyed being out in public promoting my work. In fact, I had a huge fear of public speaking, so the thought of standing on stage to promote my work and share my message was crippling. I was at a crossroads: I had to decide if I wanted to be a writer and hide behind my computer for the rest of my life, launching my books and hoping someone would find them through my limited marketing efforts, or if I wanted to get out into the world, as an author and the authority in my business, and share my message with the world and those who could benefit from what I had to offer.

And then I found a happy medium.

I started to look at my strengths and noticed that although I didn't have a desire for public speaking, I was pretty good at online marketing. I didn't mind reaching out to the masses by building my list, networking on social media, blogging, crafting newsletters, and writing emails. Before long, I found I had built my confidence to host webinars, online challenges, and coach in a group setting such as online courses and closed Facebook groups where I had grown to become the expert in my niche.

Before I knew it, I was working one-on-one with clients, doing face-to-face trainings, and in-person and group retreats.

I took baby steps to get to that stage, but you know what? *I did it.* And in the end I found I had built one hell of an empire along the way. And that's what I want for you.

If the thought of speaking engagements and promoting your work frightens you, don't close this book just yet. I'm going to show you ways you can build your empire, whether you have a desire to get out into the public eye and rub elbows, or you want to do it from the comfort of your home office, or even perhaps on the beaches of Bali on your self-funded world tour. I plan to cover as many options for you as possible in the pages ahead, so you can decide what feels right for you and then implement those ideas and skills over time, as your confidence builds.

You may choose not to implement all the strategies I offer within these pages, and that's perfectly fine. Everything I cover inside this book is not for everyone. By the time you are done reading, you will have enough tools and resources to build an empire that's specific to your needs and the needs of your business. I am just here to offer a toolbox full of ideas for you to choose from so you can utilize the ones that are right for you.

The goal here is to always be building your empire and expanding upon it. If money is an issue for you starting out, as it is for many people when they first launch a business, start with some of the free strategies I list and then add tools and resources as you can afford them, over time.

Is there an investment in some of these tools? Yes, there could be depending on what you decide to utilize. Over the years I've invested thousands upon thousands of dollars (I won't say how much!) in everything from training programs to learn how to create a webinar, to membership site plugins, to hiring business mentors to get me to the next level. Building a business isn't free and it isn't cheap. I'm sure you've heard the saying that you have to spend money to make money? Well, I believe in that statement, but I also believe we shouldn't go bankrupt building our business. Take baby steps, implement new tools over time, and as you make increasing profits, reinvest them into your business and create another product for your empire. That's how empires are built. There is no right or wrong way and it doesn't have to be done all at once. It took me time to get to where I am in my business, but if I can share the tools, resources and strategies I used to get where I am today and help my readers by taking the trial and error out of building their empire, then I can rest well at night knowing I've helped someone by sharing what has worked (and still does work) well for me.

And who knows, perhaps you and I will do a joint venture down the road and promote each other's work. The sky's the limit, but one thing is certain: You'll never learn to fly if you don't get off the ground, so let's get started, shall we?

It's time to build your empire.

CHAPTER TWO

Develop Your Brand

Before we can begin to build your empire, first we have to ensure you have established a brand for your business, one that sets you apart from the competition. Earlier I spoke about how I first branded my business as all things having to do with *Write from the Heart*. Now I've evolved from just working with aspiring authors, to also advising authors who want to build a business based on the concepts in their book; thus, I've long since graduated from being the Write from the Heart Writing Coach. Your brand may also evolve and change over time as your business grows, and you should remain open to change as it comes, but for now, let's be sure you have a solid foundation to begin building your brand. To do so, you'll need to find your target audience and create your elevator pitch geared toward that specific audience.

In this chapter, we will explore your passions and your gifts, scope out your ideal avatar and create an elevator pitch, craft your author bio and develop your unique brand, to set you apart from your competition in your area of expertise.

Explore Your Passions/Gifts

You may already have an idea for your book or business, or you might even already have a business started. If so, great, you're ahead of the game, but don't jump ahead just yet. Even if you already have an idea or *think* you have a clear vision for your business, I urge you to review this section anyway. We want to ensure your business is aligned with your passions and your purpose, and not what you think will be profitable or what has brought success to others.

So often I see the same scenario. Sally sees Josie making money hand over fist selling real estate, so Sally starts to wonder if she should be selling real estate too, especially since Josie keeps romanticizing the idea and selling her on the notion that she should get into the business. She's a sales person, after all, and a damn good one at that, so it isn't long before Sally is sold. So, what happens next? Sally sets a good chunk of time aside getting her license, finding a brokerage, and learning the ins and outs of the business while Josie continues to make sales each month, often excelling in her office as the top listing agent, getting bonus after bonus, referral after referral. Although Josie helps her good friend Sally when she can, it's ultimately up to Sally to find her own success. Sound familiar? It does for me, because that very example is based on my own personal experience in my twenties when I set out to sell real estate because I saw my best friend excelling at that vocation and I figured I could, too. Well, do I even need to tell you what happened next? I failed. I just wasn't any good at selling real estate. It wasn't *my* passion, it wasn't *my* dream, and to be quite honest with you, I don't even like sales. More importantly, it wasn't my purpose.

I wish I could say this is the only time I embarked on an entrepreneurial venture because I saw someone else meet with success, but it wasn't. In fact, in my twenties I experienced many failures as I tried to find my way in the world and discover a vocation that was right for me. No matter how hard I worked, I never found the same success as those I was following, and do you know why? I wasn't in alignment with *my* purpose. Doors just weren't opening for me; in fact, they closed more often than not. If I had known then what I know now, that would have been a good indication that I was on the wrong path, but unfortunately I didn't know any better, and I wasted valuable time chasing someone else's dream. Don't do that.

> **Follow your bliss and the universe will open doors where there were only walls.**
> **—Joseph Campbell**

It wasn't until I stopped chasing what I thought would bring me happiness and success by following what was working for others, and instead looked at what *my* gifts and passions were and then built a business doing what *I* do best that everything started lining up for me. Once I stopped ignoring my gifts and started pursuing my passions, that's when doors of opportunity started to open and the universe lined up all the resources I needed to achieve success. The right people began to show up in my life; each time I needed to take the next step or reach the next level, opportunities and resources appeared. You know why? I was finally aligned with my purpose, and the universe rewards those of us who follow our bliss and stay in alignment with our heart's true desire. Don't worry, I won't get all "woo-woo" on you here, I'll save that for another book, but if you think this is farfetched,

I urge you to take a moment to think back on your past business ventures. Write them down, as many as you can recall, and note where you found success and where you experienced failure. For your successes, I would bet that list was in line with your passions and your gifts. Where you had failure, that list was likely when you were trying to achieve success in an area when your heart just wasn't all that into it.

Now, I want you to take some time to really think about what your passions are. Set aside any ideas for your business you have or preconceived notions you've already decided on. I'm not saying you have to change your business model or throw away the dreams you've created, but I challenge you to try an exercise. Humor me, if you will.

Get out a sheet of paper, and divide it down the middle. The left side is your *passion* side. I want you to make a list of everything you love. On this side, list all your interests, not just in business, but in life, and include your hobbies. What makes you come alive? What nourishes your soul? Write those down. List as many as you can—get another sheet of paper, if necessary.

> **Don't ask what the world needs. Ask what makes you come alive, and go do it. Because what the world needs is people who have come alive.**
> **—Howard Thurman**

Once you've filled that side to completion, I want you to make a new list on the right-hand side. These are your *gifts*. Now write down everything you are good at. Where do you really excel? What comes easily to you? What are people often asking you for help with or advice on? Write down as many strengths as you can.

Now, compare both sides. Where do you see an overlap? Can you find a connection between each side? If you want to find success, if you want to build a business that makes your heart sing, I encourage you to find something that combines both your passions and your gifts. Even if it doesn't seem lucrative to you at the moment, the money will come. The universe will provide. Once you surrender to your calling, find your purpose, and pursue that which sets your soul on fire, you will be unstoppable! You will find success, because you will be in complete alignment with your purpose.

Whenever I work with an aspiring author who has several book ideas and doesn't know which one to focus on first, I have them do this exercise. It's a great way to narrow down your options. It's always best to start with the book that will not only be easiest for you to write, but will help you sustain momentum for the ongoing marketing that's required after it's published. If you're not passionate about your topic, you won't have the energy or endurance to make your book a success.

Define Your Ideal Avatar

As you begin the journey of marketing your books and services, you must create communications that attract your prospective readers and clients to you and your product. To do so, we need to scope out who your ideal client or avatar is, and then create an "Elevator Pitch," which explains the benefits and results you can offer him or her in simple statements.

Visualize an image of your ideal reader/client in your mind's eye. We will call this person your avatar. What does he or she look like? How old? What income bracket? Hobbies/interests? What age range are you targeting? Male, female, or both? Take some time to jot down as many points as you can about your ideal target client. This will be the person you market to, so you'll want a clear vision of your avatar before you proceed.

Be very specific here. For example, when it was time for me to narrow down my ideal client or reader for this book, I didn't just say, "Someone who wants to write a book." That's too vague, and let's be honest, who *doesn't* want to write a book? I specifically wanted to appeal to a market of aspiring authors and entrepreneurs with a desire to build a business on the concepts of their book. I envisioned a forward-thinking professional who doesn't go small. Someone who doesn't stop at publication and instead wants to go the extra mile. Someone who wants to begin with the book and then expand upon their message from within their book, whether that be through coaching, speaking, online marketing, or creating supporting products. My ideal client is neither male nor female, as this book applies to both, but my ideal avatar is specific, my avatar is driven by an entrepreneurial spirit.

This book cannot help the person who wants to write and publish a book just to fulfill a lifetime goal, hit publish, and then expect the readers and money to find them. This book is for the motivated authorpreneur who wants to build an empire, so I needed to get very clear about who I would speak to as I wrote this book. I created a list of attributes and then spent some time visualizing what that person epitomized. I want you to do the same. If your ideal avatar is gender specific, you may even want to give him or her a name. It will help if you can keep this person in mind while you build your brand and write your book. He is your ideal client, so you'll want to speak to him as you write, as if he were standing right in front of you.

Before you read any further, set some time aside to give this some thought and do this exercise. Once you have a clear vision of who you are marketing to, it's time to move toward crafting your elevator pitch.

Develop Your Elevator Pitch

First, take your findings from the above exercise and create a statement that clearly defines your ideal avatar. By this point, you should have a clear vision of who you are targeting, and should be able to define your avatar in just one or two sentences.

Next, describe the specific problem, interest or issue that your reader is having, in clear terms. What goal is your avatar trying to accomplish? What problems are they facing? What do they need to attain or excel at to get to the next level?

Now, think about how *you* can help your avatar. What do you have to offer that will solve their problem and deliver a solution for their success? Describe the specific, measurable result that you will help your reader to achieve by reading your book or working with you through the services you have to offer. Describe the specific convenience that you offer in helping your reader get past their challenges, and realize the results they want to achieve.

Finally, turn that information into an elevator pitch—a brief statement that defines what you have to offer, and who specifically your offer can help and targets. Your elevator pitch, or unique selling proposition, should be memorized until it rolls confidently and eloquently off your tongue, as you will be repeating it often. Each time someone asks, "What do you do?" or "What is your book about?" or "Who are your clients?" this is your opportunity to *wow* them with your elevator pitch, and it's your answer to this very question that will open doors of opportunities for speaking, teaching, and marketing your business. With this in mind, you can see why it's important we start here and complete this step before we go any further.

I'll now offer you an example of my ideal avatar and elevator pitch to get you started:

> **Ideal Avatar:** A forward-thinking author with an entrepreneurial spirit and a desire to build a business by creating companion products and services based upon the core concepts of their book.

Simply stated, right? But clear and to the point. Not just an author, not just someone who wants to write a book, but an authorpreneur, hence the name of the very book you are holding.

> **Elevator Pitch:** *Authorpreneur* helps authors and entrepreneurs build an empire based on the core concepts of their book, by creating companion products and services to support and grow their business.

See, that wasn't so hard. Two simple statements and I can clearly define my ideal avatar, and also the elevator pitch for my business. Now when someone asks, "What is your book about?" or "What is your business?" I can quickly and confidently answer without skipping a beat.

Your turn. Take some time to craft your ideal avatar and elevator pitch and practice reciting these statements until it becomes second nature. Imagine you are riding in an elevator with someone who asks what you do, or what your book is about. You'll want it to be brief, but precise and to the point. The goal here is to be as specific as possible, but relay a clear message of what you have to offer in the short amount of time it takes to ride between floors. When the bell dings and the doors open, your chance is shot. So craft a statement and memorize it. Aim for confidence and clarity.

Crafting Your Bio

Now that you've explored your passions and gifts, decided who your ideal avatar is, and created your elevator pitch, crafting your bio should come relatively easy, but take some time to perfect it, and remember to always be adding to it and tweaking it as you and your business grow and evolve.

There are many ways to write and structure a bio, but if you are struggling to write about yourself as so many of us do, here's a basic format to get you started:

To start, make a list of your accomplishments, credentials, education, and awards you've won or were nominated for. Highlight times when you've excelled in life or in business. Your bio should be a nice blend of your personal and professional achievements. Traditionally, bios were almost always written in the third person, but it's not uncommon nowadays to visit someone's "About" page on their website and see their bio written in first person, which makes it more personal and conversational. I am still a fan of the third person bio, but it's up to you which point of view you'd like to use.

I like to break this list into three sections:

Paragraph One: Most recent titles and roles. This is where you want to showcase your most recent achievements. What is your title? Are you a bestselling author? Of what book? What's your business? Feature your current status and most notable successes first.

Paragraph Two: List any special training you have, other published work, your accomplishments and awards—any relevant roles that you've held that you didn't mention in paragraph one.

Paragraph Three: Here is your chance to get personal. Share a bit about your passions, hobbies, offer an insider's view of you on a more personal level. This is where you can add a little taste of your personality and make it your own.

When you are finished, you should have both a long and short version of your bio. For the long version, keep it around 250 words. For your short bio, approximately 50-75 words is a good rule of thumb. There will be times when you will need the long version, such as in your media kit, book bios and your website's "About Me" page, and times when you will need a shorter version, such as for use in guest blogging, and on social media profile descriptions. Having both available will save you time in a crunch.

Your Unique Brand

Building your brand is like trying to find your identity; it can be tricky and is often the hardest piece of the puzzle to put in place. Your brand represents you and your business. It is an extension of your style and personality, yet it also portrays who and what you want to attract. Where I often see people struggle is in trying to develop a brand that is professional yet doesn't include *them* in it. It's important to be professional, yes, but if your brand is lacking what makes you YOU, then you are missing an opportunity to connect with your avatar. Instead of worrying about what you *think* others want to see from you, or what you believe your brand should look like, I would encourage you to take some time to find your own unique style, and then find a way to convey that style in the message for your business.

> **TIP:** One tool I like to use for mapping out a brand is Pinterest. I should maybe insert a disclaimer here warning about the addictiveness of Pinterest, so proceed with caution! It can be fun to create a branding board and then pin graphics, quotes, color pallets, fonts, and articles that appeal to you. If you decide to create a branding board with Pinterest, pin freely, without stopping to question whether something is right for your brand. But I would recommend making this board private so it can only be viewed by you. Set aside a few hours for this. Later when you go back through it, you will start to see a pattern for your individual style. Next you can create a new board to narrow down your branding, and choose the colors, fonts and graphics you're most attracted to from your first board. Are you a minimalist? Or is your style more colorful? Do you like bold colors or pastels? Do you like romantic fonts? Or is your style more edgy? How can you tie it all together for your business?
>
> Having a branding board on Pinterest is especially helpful if you decide to work with a branding expert, or designer for your website, book cover, or business materials. By sharing your branding board you are

offering a clear vision of your tastes, and this visual can aid in creating your business materials.

Once you have a clear vision of your brand, style, and elements, you'll want to incorporate it all into your business in areas such as:

- Website
- Social media headers
- Logo
- Email signature
- Business cards
- Photo shoot
- Book cover (optional)

Keeping your branding consistent across the board will help with brand recognition. You'll want to be recognizable, so it's a good idea to have a series of headshots from the same photo shoot and use them for your bio, business cards, and social media profile pictures.

Be sure to get a release from your photographer for the photos. You will need it to show you have the legal right to use the photos in your marketing, and when it's time to publish your book, your publisher will likely require a photo release for your headshot. You'll want to credit their work on the copyright page of your book as well.

For your logo, you may want to use something simple such as your signature in a script font, or you might decide to have a symbol added or to stand alone to represent your business.

Make sure your colors, fonts, headshots and photos stay consistent—from your website, to social media, to your logo, to your business cards. It should all tie together. Find your personal brand and then begin to create the elements you'll need to build your business.

We will cover website and social media creation in Chapter Four when we discuss building your author platform. For now, find your style and your unique brand, and remember to include what makes you YOU! That is what your tribe will want to see, and that is what will attract them to you in the first place.

CHAPTER THREE

Laying the Foundation

As a book coach, working with authors through the developmental phase of their ideas is something I specialize in. This will often prove to be the most beneficial point in the book-writing process, and yet it's often the same place where writers get stuck and even abandon the project in frustration.

I am going to make this process seamless for you. Through my unique coaching system, I've found a way to simplify this process, so you'll start this chapter with an idea in mind and leave with a plan of action. Even if you already have your book mapped out in your mind, or if you have your outline written or have started writing, I urge you to work through this chapter anyway, as you may develop further insights for your book. Each exercise progressively builds upon the last, so do each exercise in order.

Step One: Find Your Niche

In the last chapter when we discussed finding your gifts, I had you explore topics that you are not only passionate about, but also those in which you are gifted. If you completed the exercise, you likely found a topic that overlapped on each side. Your empire will ideally be derived from a topic that you are both passionate about *and* knowledgeable on.

What I don't want you to do is think about money at this point. Don't choose a topic that you think will make you a lot of money. Although I do believe it's important to be mindful that there is a demand for your information, we will be able to find your niche and target audience after we find your topic, and if you choose a topic you are passionate about, one that you can confidently and proudly promote to the world, your enthusiasm and high vibration will attract clients and success to you, and your passion for your topic will become the fuel that drives you to the finish line. The topic you build your empire upon should be your gift to the world, the ultimate extension of who you are.

To find your niche, keep these questions in mind:

- What topic do you know enough about to write a book on that subject?
- Can you see yourself building a business and brand around that topic?
- Do you feel passionate about that topic?
- What topics do you find yourself talking about most often?
- On what topic do people constantly ask you questions?
- What answers or advice do you find yourself repeating in relation to this topic?

The answers above will be a good indication of what a good topic for your empire might be. If you have a few topic ideas, I want you to brainstorm on each of them separately, so choose one for each brainstorming session and when you are finished, you can move on to the next.

There are dozens of ways to brainstorm and mind map, and all sorts of fancy apps and software to assist in the process, but for the sake of keeping things simple, I am going to teach you a proven technique that I've used to coach numerous students and clients from idea to publication.

Step Two: Brainstorm Your Book Idea

Grab a sheet of paper and start by writing down your main idea or premise. Next, start recording any words or phrases that come to mind. Include everything that surfaces without stopping to re-think or second-guess your ideas. Either make a list of your thoughts running down the page or start with your main concept in the center of the page in a bubble. As each new thought strikes, create another line or add each additional idea in a new bubble. Each branch that shoots off from your main idea may become a section or chapter in your book, but don't worry about structure just yet. At this point, you want to write freely whatever words or phrases enter your mind. Don't stop to second-guess yourself, just jot it all down. It may not make much sense at the time but through word association it may spark another idea, so it's important to write freely without interrupting the creative flow while brainstorming.

If you are toying with a few book ideas and are unsure of which one to choose, I would encourage you to work through this brainstorming exercise for each of your book ideas individually. When you are finished with each brainstorming session, take notice of which session flowed more freely and got you most excited. Your emotions are a roadmap for your path and purpose in life. Follow what brings you joy and excites you, and you will be more likely to meet success on the journey ahead by focusing on it. On the other hand, if you force an idea and it isn't one that's truly in your heart, you might be more likely to abandon the project.

As entrepreneurs, we have creative energy flowing through us at all times, and we often have many book ideas we'd like to pursue. You will have plenty of time to work on your other ideas, but for now, I encourage you to choose one and stick with it.

Step Three: Choose Your Topic

As mentioned above, you likely have several ideas for books you want to write or brands you'd like to create. So how do we narrow it down to just one? Here's something to keep in mind: After you publish one book, it's very likely you will publish many more, and we will discuss methods for creating additional products later in this book. But for this exercise, I want you to choose that one signature book that will ultimately become the flagship product you build your empire upon. Keep in mind, the topic you choose to write about now will become the foundation for your empire.

Even if you already have a successful business or are looking to build a business around the core concepts in your book, your book will make a nice product as an extension of you, your gifts and your brand. So take some time to figure out what your passions are, what your gifts are, and brainstorm ideas on how you can turn your passion and gifts into your life's work. If you can do that, running your business won't be "work" and it will bring you joy and satisfaction for many years to come.

Step Four: Visualize

Take a moment to find a place free of distractions and quiet your mind. I'm not asking you to meditate, although I do find meditation to be a valuable tool to unlock creativity during the writing process. For this exercise, simply get quiet and close your eyes.

I want you to envision a day in the life of your dreams. Take a moment to figure out exactly how that life looks. What do you do upon rising each morning? Do you go to an office, or do you have the luxury of working from a home office? Perhaps you don't work at all, but I doubt that's the case. You wouldn't be reading this book if there wasn't a deep-rooted longing to create a life based on your passions, so what are they? In a perfect world, how do you spend your day?

This exercise will help you get clear on what exactly you would do with your time if you could do anything your heart desires. Once you have a vision of what that is, it's a pretty good indication that you've discovered your path. Whether you visualize a day of networking with clients, online marketing, or simply writing from the privacy of your home office, taking time to envision the life you want to achieve each day will help you find success much faster. This concept is not new age, successful men have been practicing visualization techniques from time immemorial. Napoleon Hill penned *Think and Grow Rich* in 1937, and in the book he references those who succeeded with these techniques before him such as Henry Ford and Neville Goddard, by using the same core concepts.

You may even take this one step further and write out your script. Write it in detail and incorporate all the senses. Write it as if it already is in place, in present tense. When you read it each day, feel the joy and gratitude in your heart for having attained the life of your dreams. Take time each day to do this, and as you are doing it, the universe will be busy shuffling things around to align you with your true desires.

Once you make a decision, the universe conspires to make it happen.

—Ralph Waldo Emerson

Step Five: Outline

Now that you've taken some time to get clear on what you really want in life, and have brainstormed your topic to further develop your ideas, it's time to craft those ideas into a book. The best way to flesh out your ideas and create a roadmap for your writing journey is to create an outline. If you are like most of us, you just froze when you read that sentence. An *outline?* Something about the word alone takes us back to middle-school English class and causes us to lose our momentum. Don't let the thought of creating an outline kill the forward-moving progress you just worked to create in the previous exercises.

It's time to pull it all together and create a roadmap for your book-writing journey. We create an outline not to enforce structure and discipline, but as a way to help you organize your thoughts, and build a template for your book. As you're writing, there will be times when your book will likely take on a life of its own and you may veer off track from your initial outline. Resist the urge to stop the flow of creativity just because it isn't what you initially set out to create. When the book starts to develop, see where it takes you. If you lose your way, or get stuck, that's when you'll want to reference the outline to help you regroup, collect your thoughts, and get back on track.

The reason I enjoy having an outline is because I don't like to work on my book in order, and that is fine, there is no right or wrong way. To each his own. Take my experience with writing this book, for example. I started with the first couple chapters, but then I skipped ahead. I worked on what appealed to me each day. Since I had my outline to refer back to, I didn't forget about something I wanted to include in chapter three just because I jumped ahead and wrote chapters four, six and nine first. I wrote the pieces that came easily for me first, and then I went back and filled in the missing sections from my outline.

Once the book was complete, I moved chapters, took a few sections from one chapter to add to another, rewrote the intro, etc., and in the end my final product isn't an exact replica of my original outline, *but* I included everything I wanted in the book because I had the outline to help me refer back to my core intentions.

In case you are wondering what you need to include in your outline, let's take a look at some components of non-fiction books to get you started:

> **Dedication:** Adding a statement of dedication for the book is a nice touch when you want to dedicate your book in honor of someone special, or you may simply add a quote to set the tone for the pages ahead.

> **Free Bonus Gift:** A free gift that complements the information you're providing in your book that your reader must opt-in for; thus, adding your reader to your mailing list.

> **Table of Contents:** The TOC lists sections, chapter headings, and subheadings within the body of the text.

> **Foreword:** A short introduction to your book written by a third party, such as a well-known person or esteemed colleague. A Foreword is basically a credible opinion from someone else that your book is worth reading.

Preface: The Preface is written by you, the author. The goal of the Preface is to offer readers background information on who you are and how the book came to be. It should also let readers know who the book is for and what they can expect in the pages ahead.

Introduction: An Introduction to a book is often used to take the place of a Preface, because many readers commonly skip over the Preface. By labeling this section as an Introduction in lieu of a Preface, your readers may be more likely to read it.

Body of Text: Your chapters will make up the majority of your book. Each chapter should have a theme and may include subheadings or topics related to the main topic of the chapter. It's nice to include at least one story or example in each chapter to help your readers further understand the concept/topic in which you are presenting.

Conclusion: The closing chapter of the book, often summarizing what you have covered and how to tie it all together. It should leave your reader motivated and inspired to take action on what you've delivered inside the book.

Appendix: The section(s) at the end of a book that offers additional information on the topics explored in the contents of the text. A few examples of an Appendix are pages at the end of a book containing a list of other informational texts about the topic, charts, an index, or even a terminology section.

Bibliography: If you have conducted research, mentioned other books, or quoted other authors, a Bibliography acknowledges those sources.

Acknowledgments: This is where you want to thank those who had an active part in the production and publication of the book, or have supported your journey in some way.

About the Author: This is a good place to add your long author bio (the short bio will usually go on the back cover), contact information, links to social media and other published works. You may also add a headshot to this section.

Call-to-Action: This page is optional and is usually the final page a reader arrives at once finishing your book. This is a good area to add a strong call-to-action, encouraging readers to continue the journey with you. Let them know the next logical step that you'd like them to take.

The above components will give you options of what should come at the beginning and end of your book; now you just need to map out what will go in the body of the book.

Take your insights from your brainstorming session and start to put your chapter ideas in a logical order, either on paper or by using note cards. Again, don't get too hung up on structure now because you can always move chapters around later during the revision process. For now, we just want to create a roadmap as easily as possible so you can get started on the task at hand, writing your book.

For each chapter, list the topic and then add three to five bullet points for each. If I were to show you the beginning outline I created for this book, you'd see the end result didn't follow my initial ideas to a tee, but having the outline to reference ensured I included all my topics and ideas as I wrote. I marked it up and made notes of things I wanted to move and things I wanted to add. I kept a visible, hard copy of my outline on my desk during the writing process, and crossed off each section as I included it, like you would a to-do list. I don't know about you, but I have a feeling of accomplishment each time I complete a task and am able to cross something off my to-do list. Using this process while writing my book proved to be motivational for me, and I truly believe it helped me complete my book much quicker than I'd first determined. I looked forward to completing a section and crossing it off my list each day, and it became a goal to cross off a section each day until the book was complete.

Let's keep this simple for the sake of being productive. Take your findings from the previous exercises and create a loose outline for your book. Easier said than done, right? It doesn't have to be hard, so let's not over-complicate it.

First, look at your brainstorming session. You can probably see how certain topics are clustered together to form a potential chapter. For now, start separating your ideas by chapter, without thinking of a logical order. As mentioned, you may want to use index cards for this, with each chapter topic at the top of the card with three to five bullet points listed on what you will include within that chapter.

Once you have as many chapters as you can think of, add a few bullets for your Introduction, Conclusion, and About the

Author page (refer back to the bio you created from Chapter Two). That's a good start for now; later you can add the Acknowledgments, Endorsements, Appendixes, Bonus Gift, and a strong Call-to-Action page to drive traffic to your other products and services such as a coaching/mentoring program, companion products, or an online course or membership site. But let's not get ahead of ourselves just yet.

Step Six: Create a Plan of Action

If you know the type of book you've set out to write, and you know the average word count of that style of book, then you can decide a date when you would like to have your first draft finished, and we can estimate your target daily word count.

The first step in finding your target daily word count is setting a goal for the final word count of your manuscript. Most nonfiction books range anywhere from 25,000-50,000 words. If you are creating a product for your business, aiming for 40,000 words is a good goal. (This book is 45,000 words, while *Self-Publishing Success* is closer to 35,000.)

For example, I estimated my final word count for this book at 40,000 before I began, and once complete, the first draft was at 39,689 words. So as you can see I stayed true to my goal, but you may go over or fall a bit short, and that is fine. After editing and revisions, my final draft was just over 45,000 words. You could even look at the page count of this book and the thickness and decide if you'd like more or less for your own book. Keep in mind, this won't be an exact measurement because all books vary depending on font style and size, spacing, etc., but this will at least give you an idea of what a 45,000-word book looks like.

Now that you have a goal for your final word count in mind, you can easily set a goal for your target daily word count, but first, you will need to set a completion date for your first draft. Notice I said your first draft, and not a completion date for your book. I will ask you to write your first draft in a condensed block of time, and then spend a decent amount of time revising, editing and crafting the final product. The reason is this: If you set out to write a book in a shorter time frame, you are less likely to stop the flow of creativity each day and go back and edit as you write. When you write freely, you unlock the flow of creativity and silence the ego—that voice that second-guesses your word choices and tells you your last line was crap and you need to rewrite it. If you can, silence those voices and write unencumbered each day, knowing that there will be plenty of time for revision in the next draft. In turn, you will write your first draft much faster and it will likely flow more easily.

Each time you stop to second-guess word choices or change something you just wrote, you stop the creative flow, and it takes approximately 20 minutes to get back into that flow. If you are like me, you may only set aside an hour or two each day to work on your book, so you can't afford to stop that creative process. That's why it's important to resist the urge to edit as you go, and write swiftly and freely during your dedicated writing time. There is a time for revision, but it should be scheduled separately from your writing time.

It's up to you how much time you want to allow yourself for creating your book. This is the foundation for your business, and although it shouldn't be rushed (you want to put out a high-quality product), you shouldn't offer yourself too much time when deciding on a completion date. The goal is to get the book done so you can start creating all the companion products and programs that go along with it, so I would urge you to set a shorter time frame while still making it realistic.

For a non-fiction book, I like to set a goal of 90 days. Again, you are welcome to take longer if you feel you need to, but I would urge you to set an immediate deadline and then work diligently toward it each day. This will keep the momentum going for your project, increasing your probability of achieving success much faster.

7-Day Challenge to Increase Writing Speed and Unlock Creativity

Are you up for it? I challenge you to try this for one week. If you will commit to this exercise for an hour each day for seven days, I am willing to bet you will not only increase your writing speed, but you will find your writing is far more creative and heartfelt than ever before.

Ready to give it a try? Here's how to do it:

- **Keep a notepad near your computer or dedicated writing space.** You may also elect to use an app on your phone or computer. There are many websites and apps that you can use to record your daily word count, but for the sake of keeping it simple, I suggest starting with a notepad for this 7-Day Challenge.

- **You will need to time yourself for one hour each day.** Be sure to schedule your writing time for when you will be free of distractions. You may choose to leave your house and find a small cafe or park where you can write. I tend to do my daily writing early in the morning when I'm the only one awake in my home. Schedule your daily writing time into your calendar for one week and commit to 60 minutes of writing during each session. Now, you may choose to continue to write beyond the hour, and if so, by all means ... write on! But I want you to break at the one-hour point to record your word count. For this you will need a timer.

- **Use a stopwatch, hourglass, kitchen timer**–whatever works. Something to alert you of the one-hour mark. I use the stopwatch on my iPhone. You may even use an alarm clock. You will likely be deeply engrossed in your writing so be sure that whatever gadget you choose will send an alert when your 60 minutes are up.

- **Record your daily word count on your notepad.** The goal is to not only meet your current word count, but surpass it by a few words each day. Consequently you will begin to write or type faster and you will get out of your head and write from your heart. And when you write from the heart, that's when the magic happens!

- **Tips for success:** Focus on one project for the duration of the 7-Day Challenge, such as a book, short story, or an article. Resist the urge to jump from project to project during this challenge.

Each day, stop writing mid-sentence so when you pick it back up the following day you will not stall when trying to get started. By stopping mid-sentence today, you are setting yourself up for success tomorrow.

Turn off your spell/grammar check during your hour of uninterrupted writing. Don't worry, you can turn it back on when it's time to revise and edit. Oftentimes those red lines under our words can be a distraction and many find it hard to resist the urge to correct as they go.

Finding a Target Daily Word Count

Now that you know how many words you write per hour, you can use this information to better plan your writing time; but first, we need to establish your target daily word count.

A simple formula to find your target daily word count:

How many words do you estimate your book will have upon completion? _____

Set a goal. How many days of writing will you have? _____

Target Daily Word Count Formula

Estimated   final   word   count_____divided by_____days = _____ **Target Daily Word Count**

Example:

Annie plans to write a how-to non-fiction book about productivity in the workplace. She estimates her book will be approximately 40,000 words once complete. She is setting a goal to have her first draft finished in 90 days.

40,000 words divided by **90 days** = **444 words per day**

There you have it! Annie's **Target Daily Word Count** *is 444 words.*

Take it one step further: Annie records her word count each day, so she knows she averages 1000 words per hour of uninterrupted writing. Looking at her target daily word count, she now can determine she needs to write approximately 30 minutes each day to stay on schedule to complete her first draft in 90 days. If she falls off track and skips a day, she will double her target daily word count the following day to catch up.

Do you think you can commit to 30 minutes of writing each day? If so, you could complete a 40,000 word manuscript in 90 days!

If you completed the seven-day challenge, you know how many words you average per hour, so if you write 1,000 words per hour, for example, and your target daily word count is 444, you know that if you write for an hour instead of 30 minutes, you can complete the book in half the time, meeting your goal much faster.

Now that you've reviewed the formula, doesn't completing your book in 90 days seem more attainable? Again, you are free to choose a time frame that fits your lifestyle and schedule, but I'm a firm believer in setting an immediate goal and then working hard each and every day until reaching its completion.

A goal without a plan is just a wish.
—Antoine de Saint-Exupéry

Step Seven: Implement Your Plan

Now it's time to map out your book writing journey. This is where you will need self-discipline and focus, because your book isn't going to write itself and it will take dedication and a strong commitment to realize your goal of finishing your book.

You've found your target daily word count, so be sure to add your completion date to your calendar. Write it on a post-it note and stick it on your computer. Write it down and post it in as many places as you need to keep you on track. This is where it will become important not to lose your momentum. Give yourself an accelerated time frame. Here's why: If you set out to write your book in over six months or a year, you become lackadaisical about your book. You won't keep that momentum you need to propel you forward and on to its completion. Besides, you want to build a business around the core concepts of this book, so you need to get it done quickly. There are some who will argue that a book should not be rushed and I agree, if you are setting out to write a memoir or your life's story. But we are talking about a book that you want to be the base of your biz. It's the first of many products you will create in your area of expertise; therefore, it is most important that you finish it within the dedicated time frame you determine.

If you think you need six months, then take them. But I wrote the first edition of this book in less than two months. You can too. At the beginning of January of 2016, I set out to plan my year. I had been hosting my online course, the Write from the Heart 8-Week Book Writing Intensive, for over a year, launching it with three live rounds, and I was ready to rebrand myself and my business. I wanted to move toward not only working with aspiring authors, but to delve into the business side of it (mainly because I listened to what my clients and students wanted and needed), because it's not enough just to write and publish a book and wait for the sales to start flowing in. You need to implement a strong marketing plan to succeed, and if you want to make real money off your book, frankly, the bulk of your money won't come from book sales. Why the sad face? I'm just being honest here. Yes, you will make royalties off your book sales and you may sell some from your website and events for even more profits, but the real money is going to come with the programs and products your readers want after they read your book–the back-end offers. Those that support your business and your message.

So that is why we must get the book finished as soon as possible, because after all, you have an empire to build.

So, decide on a date and stick to it. I say 90 days is more than enough time, it's generous even. Count 90 days out on your calendar and write this down: first draft complete. I'm not talking about having your polished manuscript ready for publication; I'm talking about your first draft. And your first draft is really just getting all those thoughts from inside your head down on paper. It's likely going to be a mess when you are finished, and that's OK. If you are like me, you will write your book out of order and have to go back and fill in the blanks and move things around. I'm not asking for perfection in 90 days, I'm asking you to complete a first draft, which is the foundation of what your book will become. We will polish, revise, move, add, and delete later. In your first draft, just get the words and ideas from within you out onto the paper or computer screen. We will discuss ways to improve upon your book later; for now I want you to pick a completion date, and stick with it.

I'm writing a first draft and reminding myself that I'm simply shoveling sand into a box so that later I can build castles.

—Shannon Hale

Now that you have a completion date set, and you know what your target daily word count is, it's time to get busy on your business. You have a job to do, and possibly one of the most important products you will create in your business is your book. Although you have a tight deadline, be mindful to create a high-quality product. This book is an extension of you, after all!

You'll want to have a conversation with your family, friends and loved ones to let them know you are writing a book and you are dedicated and serious about meeting your deadline. Ask them to respect your wishes and allow you time to work on your book over the next 90 days. I know what you are thinking, you have to get the kids to and from school, go to their sporting events, cook the meals, and perhaps you still have a full-time job. Guess what? We *all* have busy lives, and when you want something bad enough, you make the time. This is where you will have to get creative with your schedule. Get up an hour earlier, stay up an hour later, or write on your lunch break if you must, but it is up to you to find the time to write your book.

If you really want to do something, you'll find a way. If you don't, you'll find an excuse.

—Jim Rohn

Excuses be gone! In my 8-Week Book Writing Intensive, I set out to coach a group of writers through the book-writing process in an 8-week time frame. The goal was to find a target daily word count and stick to it, and make up for lost writing days when needed. If you fell behind, you'd work extra hard the following day to catch up. It was an extreme commitment and I began to notice a pattern. A few weeks into the Intensive, I started getting emails and messages from my students, talking about what came up in their lives and why they felt they were falling behind. It was the same old story: I'm just *so* busy it's hard to find the time to get my daily writing done, and so on, and so on … .

Listen, I'm busy, too. Extremely busy, actually. But when I set out to write this book, I got up at 5am every day to get my hour of writing in *before* I started my day. There were days when life did get in the way, and I did fall behind in my word count—I'm not perfect, I am human, it's going to happen. But I was mindful of how far I was falling behind, so there were Saturdays when I would have to cancel plans with family and friends to catch up on the word counts I missed throughout the week. I had a deadline. I had a plan, and by God, I was going to meet it.

When you set out to write a book, it almost has to consume your life while you are writing it. It has to be the first thing you think about when you wake up in the morning and the last thing on your mind when you go to sleep. You must take time each day to visualize the finished product, staying focused and motivated toward reaching your goals. Let that book take over your life until the first draft is finished. And then you can take a break, put it aside, and reward yourself for all your hard work. Yes, once your first draft is finished I want you to put it aside and not look at it for at least a week or so. You've worked hard, now go out and play! Reward yourself, spend time with your family and friends, maybe take a trip somewhere, and finally, take a deep breath and reflect on your accomplishment.

I ask you to set it aside and reward yourself for your hard work for two reasons: 1. I am a firm believer in balance; work hard, play hard. 2. I want you to go back to your first draft with fresh eyes before you begin the revision process and craft your second draft. After a week of not looking at your writing, you will see it in a new light. And then it's time to review, revise, and create the second draft.

7 Self-editing Tips to Polish Your Writing:

1. **Always edit with fresh eyes.** Once you've finished your first draft, it's a good idea to put it away for a week or

two before you begin the self-editing process. As mentioned, take some time to relax and recharge your battery. You will come back to your project rejuvenated and ready to tackle the self-editing process with fresh eyes and renewed motivation.

2. **Read it aloud.** Chances are you will hear what your eyes did not see as you say the words out loud. Take note of where you stumble while reading your first draft. These are the areas you may want to consider rewriting. Any sentence you have to read twice is most likely an area that needs attention. And if you stumble, chances are your readers will, too. Be mindful of longer run-on sentences that may be exhausting to unravel for readers. Tip: You can also have Microsoft Word read your manuscript to you through the Read Aloud feature.

3. **Eliminate.** Make your writing more concise and easier to read by eliminating unnecessary words and unneeded prepositions. See which words you can omit without losing the clarity of the sentence. Extraneous words to watch for are: that, just, very, really and some.

   Watch for weak, passive language such as: the 'ly' words, 'to be' verbs, especially when used with 'ing' words.

4. **Perform a line-edit.** Edit each line on its own and in context, then each paragraph and each section. One trick is to edit each section out of order and then go back and look at the piece as a whole.

5. **Watch for repetition.** Use a thesaurus to replace repetitive words with synonyms. A thesaurus can be a writer's best friend and often it is built into most writing programs. If you are using Microsoft Word, click the Review

tab from the Toolbar to find it. There are many free online thesaurus sites you can use as well.

6. **Perform a spelling and grammar check.** Use discretion when utilizing the grammar check tool in Microsoft Word. Be mindful of suggested grammar corrections that can cause you to lose your unique writing voice. For example, sentence fragments are sometimes used to gain an effect. Your grammar checker will likely advise against all sentence fragments, but sometimes they are necessary. Use discretion. Did you catch what I did there?

   NOTE: The most accurate grammar checkers I've found are Grammarly and Pro Writing Aid. They are by far my favorite online writing tools, but still, far from perfect. They each offer a limited free option, but I prefer the paid subscription that can be added as a plugin to my web browser's toolbar to check all my writing as I type, whether that be in an email, in a blog post, or even a post on social media. With their paid memberships, you can edit more pages of writing at a time, perfect for copying and pasting chapters of your book as you self-edit. Over time, their suggestions may even help to improve your writing, but a word of caution: it's not foolproof and should not be used in place of professional editing. With any software, sometimes it's just plain wrong.

7. **Avoid Clichés.** Clichés exist on all levels of writing, from ideas as a whole to phrases, and even individual words, when used under certain conditions. Question what sounds familiar, because it probably is. Ask yourself if you've heard or seen that idea/series of words before.

Spend some time reviewing and revising your manuscript and cleaning it up as you craft your second draft. Once it's polished and finished, and you think it is the best it can be, then it's time to hire an editor. There are different types of editors you can work with. Let's break down your options below:

> **Beta Readers**—A non-professional who will review your book with the intent of looking over the material to offer feedback on overall flow and structure. A word of caution here: beta readers are not explicitly proofreaders or editors, but can serve in that context if they have the skills and knowledge. However, they are offering their overall opinion of your work, so I would urge you to choose a beta reader who is outside your immediate circle of friends and family so you receive a non-biased opinion, and take their feedback with a grain of salt if they are not professionally trained or are not your target audience. I personally opt against using beta readers and work primarily with professional editors, but that is a personal choice each writer must make.

> **Book/Writing Coach**—If you feel you need enforced accountability, some hand holding, or direction during the book-writing process, you may want to hire a writing or book coach to work with you. Your coach will help you develop your outline, structure your book and hold you accountable through each step of the process.

> **Developmental Editors**—Like a writing coach, your developmental editor will work closely with you through the creation of your book, but will delve much deeper

by looking for story arc, character development, plot, theme, context—many of the elements that are important in a work of fiction. But you are writing a non-fiction book, so it may be more cost effective to seek out a writing coach if you'd like some additional help and accountability as developmental editors can be costly.

Copy Editor—This is the most common editor you will work with, especially when crafting a non-fiction book. Before you send your manuscript over to a copy editor, you'll want to ensure it is the best it can be in your eyes. Clean up your punctuation and grammar to the best of your ability. Be sure you've performed the self-editing tasks mentioned in the prior section. Your editor doesn't expect you to have perfect punctuation and grammar, that is why you are hiring them, after all, but they should not be writing or rewriting your book for you. Give it your best effort to craft a book that you are proud of *before* sending it to your editor. Then you can let them work their magic and help to make it even stronger. They will look for discrepancies your eyes may not catch, watch for redundancies, and they are trained professionals so they know all the rules as far as what should be capitalized or not, proper punctuation, grammar, dialogue, etc.

Professional editing is mandatory. I cannot iterate this enough. It doesn't matter if you are an English major, a New York Times bestselling author, or a professional editor yourself–you should not edit your own work. After you've looked at your own writing while crafting your book, your eyes will naturally skip over errors, and besides, it's always a wise idea to get a second opinion on your work from a professional whose goal is to improve your writing. Your family and friends will not make ideal editors for your work. Often they are afraid of hurting your feelings, or worse, there might be some underlying envy and you could be led astray. Getting feedback from a third party who is not emotionally invested in your work is priceless.

Proofreader: A proofreader will check your manuscript for spelling, grammar and punctuation. It's a good idea to have your final manuscript proofread prior to publication, after you've received the suggested changes from your editor and you craft your final draft. If you've added a considerable amount of content, you may want to have your manuscript edited again, but if you've only made a few changes or additions, this would be a good time to bring in a proofreader to catch any final typos.

Spend a good amount of time crafting the final draft of your book. This is the flagship product for your business, the base of your empire, so give it your best effort and create a high-quality book that is a nice representation of you and your brand. When you feel you are ready, it's time to move on to the publishing process, which we will cover in Chapter Six. In the meantime, you'll want to start building your author platform and your list now so that you have an audience to promote your book to upon publication, and that's what we'll cover in the following chapters.

CHAPTER FOUR

Building Your Platform

So you want to build an empire, eh? Before we can build the empire, we must first build a solid platform and work our way up from there. It all starts with your platform, likely one of the most important aspects of being an author. But what does that mean ... *author platform?*

Once your book is complete and you publish, then what? If you think your readers are going to come seek you out or are going to stumble upon your book, I'm here to tell you, it doesn't work like that. You may think, oh, my publisher will market my book for me. Uh, no. Your publisher may join you in some marketing, but the majority of marketing efforts are all your own.

I'm often asked by my clients, "When should I start building my platform?" My answer to them is simple: "The moment you decide you want to write a book." Notice I didn't say when you start writing, but rather when you *decide* you want to write. You might be wondering why you would want to start building an author platform before you even start writing. Simply stated:

Finding your tribe takes time, as does gaining their trust, often more time than it takes to write the book.

> **Getting a book published does NOT equate to readership. You must cultivate a readership every day of your life, and you start TODAY. Audience development doesn't happen overnight—and it's a process that continues for as long as you want to have a readership. It shouldn't be delayed, postponed, or discounted for one minute.**
>
> **—Jane Friedman**

Your tribe is that group of people who resonates with you, follows your lead, and trusts the information you share with them. Over time, you will build more and more trust and your tribe will expand. I will give you an example.

In 2012 I decided that I wanted to work with writers. I wasn't a published author as of yet, but I knew I wanted to write books in the spiritual genre. At the time I was doing a lot of soul-searching and inner work, and without consciously knowing it, I started to build my tribe. I began with an idea to build a website where writers could register and share their writing for free within a like-minded community. In February 2012, Spiritual Writers Network was born, and in just over a month I had over 1,000 writers registered on the site.

As a way to expand the reach, I created a coordinating Facebook page for SWN, which quickly grew to over 14K fans. I dabbled a little with Twitter and made a coordinating Twitter page as well, but I put the majority of my efforts into maintaining the website and staying active on Facebook. Not long after that I started my own radio show, *Write from the Heart*. I interviewed a different author each week and gave them a platform on which to share their messages. Can you see what was happening? I was building my tribe within the writing community, growing my mailing list and mailing a weekly newsletter, staying active on social media, hosting my own radio show and doing interviews on other radio shows as well. I even had a digital monthly magazine I nurtured for a year before I retired it.

By the time I released my book, I had a tribe composed of a targeted audience who trusted me and my message, and was ready to purchase my book upon publication. But there's more. I then went on to build an online course based on the teachings in my book, and now I offer coaching, courses, workshops, and other companion products in addition to my books.

So you see, instead of thinking about building your tribe as a way to sell your book upon publication, it's so much more than that. It's a way to build a dedicated fan base made up of those who will follow you for years to come and also purchase many of the other products you launch along the way.

Long ago I had an idea for a book, now I have a high-volume network of writers, a self-publishing company, a successful coaching business, courses, retreats, workshops, speaking engagements, and much more. I never set out to do all those things; they just unfolded as I evolved. And once you are a published author many possibilities will start to unfold for you as well. Doors will open, and opportunities will present themselves. You won't stop at one book. Well, you might, but I doubt it. It's too easy nowadays to get your books published and out into the world to sit back and only write one book. I'd be willing to bet you will keep writing, and before long you will have many products and services to promote and market. But who are you going to market to if you don't start building your platform today?

Without further ado, let's start building your platform!

Website/Blog

One of the first and possibly most important components of your platform will be your website. This will not only house your products and services in one convenient place, but it will also serve as an extension of you and your brand and what you have to offer. Your readers may Google you as an author while reading your book, and if you are smart you will drive traffic to your website from within your book (more on this later).

You don't have to be tech savvy to have a website, you can always hire the services of a web designer to create it and someone to maintain it, but having a website for your business in this day and age is mandatory, so whether you decide to DIY or outsource it, take that step first. However, if you do decide to build it yourself, you'll need to be somewhat fluent in design to develop a quality site. Your website is an extension of you and your business so you want it to look sharp and professional. When I look back on some of my earlier websites I'm absolutely mortified. What's more, I thought they looked good, back in the day!

As I've mentioned, I believe in a lean startup, which means not spending more than you can afford while building your empire, so if this means creating your own website on Weebly or Wix, that's an OK start; however, a WordPress or Squarespace website will offer a more professional feel. I used WordPress for over ten years before switching over to Squarespace, which I prefer for their functionality, ease of design, listed building tools, and I absolutely love their cover pages and navigation bars that offer opt-ins for my visitors. My list has grown astronomically since I implemented these tactics. For an idea of what I am talking about, head over to shandatrofe.com and transcendentpublishing.com and check out my websites—both built on Squarespace.

Before you can build your website, you'll need to choose a domain that parallels with your author name or brand. Although I've had many websites, my main hub has always been www.shandatrofe.com. When someone Googles my author name (as they will once you begin writing and publishing books), this is the website I want them to find since it includes my books, products and services. Yes, I also have a website for my self-publishing company, but that's an established business that deserves its own site.

It doesn't matter if you brand yourself as a business name or your author name, but one thing I highly recommend, if you go with your business name, you may want to buy your author name as a domain as well, and point it to your business website so you can be found easily in online searches.

Since I also have a website for Transcendent Publishing, I make sure my website visitors can access it from my author site, where they are linked in my bio and on my contact page. Over time as your brand evolves, it is possible that you may have more than one site, but for now, I want you to focus on one site that can be your main hub for your business and your empire. A one-stop-shop, if you will. Ideally, if you can keep it in one spot, it will require less work and maintenance down the road, so I highly recommend having one principal place that is the perfect representation of you and your brand to house all your products and services.

Once you decide on a domain, or domains, if you decide to buy both your business name and your author name, use a registry service such as GoDaddy.com to see if your domain is available. This is likely where you'll have to get creative and try different variations of your ideal domain if yours is taken. You may opt to try a different extension such as .net, .biz, .info, .co, etc. if your preferred domain is taken. While .com is the optimal choice, sometimes it's just not available. Try to steer clear of .org and .edu as those are reserved for non-profits and learning institutions. If you can't find a variation of your name, you can use your business or brand name instead, or buy both, as mentioned above, and point your author name to redirect to your business name.

Once you have established your domain, you'll want to find website hosting. Although GoDaddy will offer to host your domain as well, I don't recommend it. Instead, use a hosting service such as BlueHost or HostGator for web hosting if you're building a Wordpress site, and then follow their directions to point your domain from its registry to your new hosting plan. Whichever website hosting you choose will have detailed instructions on how to do this, and if you choose a reputable company you'll find they have excellent customer service reps to help you should you have the need. I used BlueHost for web hosting for Spiritual Writers Network because that was a WordPress site. For my other websites, Squarespace offers hosting built-in, and it was easy to connect my third party domain on their platform.

Now that you have your domain and hosting, it's time to choose a template and design. I personally like the cleanliness and ease of access of a horizontal navigation bar, but this is your website and you should choose a design that appeals to you.

Once you install a theme you can start the design process by changing colors, uploading plugins, adding sidebar widgets and pages if you use WordPress. Most of this is built-in if you use Squarespace, so you have options, and I urge you to research all your options before you decide on a platform. While I won't go into the design aspect here (this is where you will want to incorporate the services of a branding expert or web designer if it's not your forte), I will share which pages to add to your website to get you started:

Home: This is the main page your viewers will likely land on once they find your site, so it's your chance to wow them. This is a good place to add a welcome message and point to other areas of your site for easy navigation.

Many people opt to have their blog set as their home page as well, so if you have an active blog with valuable content that's relevant to your business, showcasing your articles on your home page may be a viable option for you; however, it's not what I prefer.

About: This is a page where your website visitors will find out more about you and/or your business. Add that bio we worked on earlier here, with a professional headshot from a photographer. List your credentials, boast your accomplishments—this area is all about you, or if you are building a business website, all about your business.

Blog: I would highly recommend adding a blog to your website, which is another reason I recommend WordPress or Squarespace, for their blogging features.

Blogging is a great way to drive traffic to your website through Search Engine Optimization (SEO), and by sharing your articles on social media. If you do add a blog to your website, be consistent with your content schedule. You can write several blog posts in advance and schedule them to publish at a later date on a blogging schedule of your choice: weekly, bi-weekly, or monthly. You'll want to include some SEO to your blog by adding keywords, but I'm not going to break down the science of blogging here.

TIP: Years ago it was popular to promote affiliate products on your blog as a way to monetize it and create extra income from your blogging efforts. There was a time when blogs were filled with ads and affiliate links, and the blogger added SEO to drive traffic to their site with the intention of making money from affiliate products and clicks on Google ads. Does that work? For some, but not as well as it once did. What's more lucrative is to create your own products to promote on your blog such as eBooks, online courses, PDF downloads, and even some physical products of your own. Why would you want to send your precious website visitors elsewhere to make a sale? You are an authorpreneur and this is *your* empire! Why not create companion products and display them on your site in lieu of affiliate products? You will make far more in the long run by selling to your tribe than by sending them elsewhere. Now, I'm not saying you shouldn't partake in joint ventures and promote affiliate products you believe in, but if your principal goal is to monetize your site, the days of adding affiliate links and Google AdSense ads are behind us. Promoting your own products is where it's at!

Products/Services: On this page you'll want to list the services and products you offer. As your business grows you will likely have many products, so you may need to add a shopping cart to your website for eCommerce to sell your products over time. If you sell digital products or online courses, you can sell them as downloads on your website, or you may opt to redirect them to a webinar, sales page or order form to make the purchase, as I do through my ClickFunnels account. With either option, you can collect payment directly on your website or direct it elsewhere—the choice is yours. NOTE: You can also separate your products and services by creating an additional page: Work with Me, and listing your business services there instead.

Contact: This area will usually contain a form that visitors can fill out to contact you, or you can simply link it to an email address. You may also opt to add links to any other websites you may have along with links to your social media pages.

> **NOTE:** Try not to use a Gmail or Yahoo address for business. Although I have a Gmail address for my personal use, and oftentimes clients who are referred to me through friends or loved ones are given that email, you should try to redirect everyone to your business email address. When you purchase your domain, you will likely get email access

along with it, or there may be a small monthly fee. It is worth it! You'll want info@yourdomain.com or yourname@yourdomain.com, but not yourname@ gmail.com. I've allowed one too many clients to get comfortable accessing me through my personal accounts, and now it's like pulling teeth to bring them over to my business address. Try not to cross that line or you will find yourself checking several email accounts each day, when you could easily check only one for business matters, which ultimately looks more professional.

If you've followed these steps you now have a three-to-five-page website! That's more than enough to get you started. Your website will grow and evolve over time, as your business grows. But for now, aim for the basics so you have a professional-looking hub that is a good representation of you and an extension of your brand for your people to find you.

Create Your Mailing List

I know I said the website was possibly the most important component, but it is really your mailing list; however, you can't build your list without a website, so we are moving in a logical order. Take note, though, this is the most important step for building your empire, because without your list, you have no tribe. Sure, you can have social media followers or YouTube subscribers, but your list is your sales machine. It is the love line that connects you to your readers, clients, fans— your people. Plus, you own it, so if your social media platform shuts down or disappears one day, you'll still have access to your subscribers.

In whatever venture you partake in to promote your business, whether online or through live events, you'll want to be driving traffic to your website. Once readers land on your website, you'll want to add them to your list through either a sidebar form or a pop-up form containing an opt-in. We will cover opt-ins as a way to entice website visitors to sign up for your list shortly, but for now I want you to get your list set up. For this, you have options. Here are a few and their pros and cons:

Beginner - MailChimp: This is a good place to start because they have a free option. At the time of writing this book it was free for up to 2,000 email subscribers. From what I understand, MailChimp has quality customer service, is easy to use, and integrates easily with other online software, but does not tolerate affiliate links if you plan to do any affiliate marketing or joint ventures.

Intermediate - Aweber: It's what I used for years for Spiritual Writers Network and it works great. However, I paid a substantial fee. When I signed up for Aweber several years ago, it was $19 per month. Over time, that fee increased to $49 per month due to the size of my list (not a bad problem to have!), but it was well worth it.

Advanced - ConvertKit: This is what I currently use because of their advanced features, tagging options, and ability to automatically remove subscribers from certain email sequences after they've made a purchase or completed a desired action. ConvertKit has many bells and whistles, and they even offer suggestions for setting up your email sequences for success, telling you which email in the sequence should be informational, and which should be a warm or hard sell. This is an ideal feature for a newbie to implement online marketing; however, there is a bit of a learning curve.

There are many others such as Active Campaign (a top choice with most online marketers), Drip, Constant Contact and Get-Response, to name a few, but I would recommend one of the three listed above as my top picks, although I would also urge you to do your research and choose the email management system that's right for you and your business.

Once you have decided on an email management system, you are ready to create a form and install it. In the beginning, you may create a form that simply says, "Subscribe to my newsletter," but as time goes on you will want to add an enticing opt-in or freebie to give away in exchange for an email address, which I highly recommend. We will go over that in greater detail later, but for now, aim to get a form on your site where your visitors can sign up and be added to your list.

When you visit someone's website you will often see a sign-up for their newsletter in the sidebar or in the footer. You can even set it to pop-up when someone visits your site.

> **TIP:** While you are building your site, it's a good idea to create a landing page with a form to start collecting subscribers to your list, even before your website is ready. You can use the homepage of your website for this, or ClickFunnels has many landing page templates, and ConvertKit has the built in option to add landing pages, which is a nice perk. They will even host the page for you!

Once you have set up your mailing list and you begin to add subscribers, you'll want to consistently send valuable information out to your list. You don't want to hound your subscribers with only programs and offers that will cost money, or only mail out to your list when you have something for sale. While you will be sending offers to them from time to time to announce your book launch or the enrollment of a new program you are offering, in between your offerings you'll want to provide value to your subscribers. Each time you write a blog post relevant to your business, share a link to the article with your subscribers and offer them a teaser of what they will find inside. They subscribed to your list because they are interested in your area of expertise, so if you are always providing relevant and cutting-edge information for free that will help them, they will be more likely to buy from you when you do propose an offer, and less likely to unsubscribe. It's a good rule of thumb to stick to the eighty-twenty rule here. Eighty percent value, twenty percent selling. Some even try to keep it to ninety-ten.

A little later we will discuss advanced techniques for adding a series of autoresponders when someone signs up for your list, offering a few freebies and products of value to establish trust with your newfound follower.

Social Media

You've got your website and you have your form installed and your list set up, now to drive traffic there. That is the battle. There are many ways of driving traffic to your website, and we will cover many ideas throughout this book, but one simple tool you can use to drive traffic to your website is to use social media.

There are many social media platforms to choose from, including:

- Facebook
- Twitter
- Instagram
- Pinterest
- LinkedIn
- GoodReads
- YouTube
- TikTok
- Snapchat

The list goes on and on …

If you were to stay consistently active on each of these platforms, your day would be consumed by social media, and I don't recommend that. Not if you want to get anything else done, anyway. My recommendation would be to choose two or three that you like and focus your energy there. Although I have set up my GoodReads account along with my Twitter, I don't spend much time there. My more concentrated efforts are focused on Facebook and Instagram, where my ideal reader/avatar is hanging out. My suggestion is to sign up for a few and take a couple of days to try out each of them. See which ones you like and stick to those.

For me, I used to schedule my social media time into my day just as my writing time. Now, I outsource the service to my social media manager to free up even more valuable time in my day. Social media can be addicting, especially in the beginning, and although it's a valuable tool for networking and driving traffic to your list, it can also be counterproductive when trying to build a business. Setting aside dedicated time for social media will help you stay consistent, and also keep you from getting sucked in to the online world of drama and countless hours of scrolling through the news feeds. However, there's something to be said for relationship building and offering value posts and comments where you can allow your expertise to shine, so some time spent on social media is necessary.

On Facebook, you can schedule a time and date for each post so you don't need to be active for the post to go live. You can also use programs like Hootsuite or Later to schedule all your social media posts, and they will publish them on your behalf.

Each platform has their own algorithm, and they are constantly changing. For example, at the time of writing this book, Facebook currently only shows your posts to a small percentage of your followers because they want you to pay to promote your posts on your business page. The more your followers interact and engage with your page, the more they will see your posts. That's why you should always be encouraging interaction by asking thought-provoking questions in your posts, and sharing a graphic with your posts also attracts attention, so be sure to add that visual.

The posts where I include a graphic or video and encourage interaction get the most likes and shares, and once your posts start getting shared around Facebook there's a chance they can go viral. This is why you should consider creating your own social media graphics. You can use a free online software such as Canva or PicMonkey to create graphics, add sayings or quotes, and at the bottom be sure to add your social media handle or website. When that post starts getting shared across cyberspace, you will have your name and your contact info on it, and be sure to keep the colors and design consistent with your branding. Consistency is key!

If you like to blog, Pinterest is a must. Start a few boards that are consistent with your brand and area of expertise. Share pins and build those boards, and once you start your blog, pin your articles there as well. You can easily make enticing Pinterest graphics for free using Canva, and when someone clicks on your graphic to learn more, they will be redirected to your website. This can also be used to sell your books, products and services.

Depending on who your ideal reader/avatar is, that will dictate where you focus your marketing efforts on social media. While a headhunter who is writing a book for his business may find LinkedIn the most beneficial place to spend his time connecting with corporate professionals, a weightloss coach might find that her avatar spends more time on TikTok or Instagram. Know your ideal reader, and figure out which platforms they prefer.

YouTube

YouTube can be a valuable resource to drive traffic to your website, and your list. We'll go over this more later, but I'd also like to emphasize that when you are in the platform-building stage, you may want to spend some time creating a YouTube channel. You can link to your website or list, and add some relevant keywords to each video description to help with SEO and ranking. Video is hot right now, and what better way to offer your viewers an inside look at your teaching style and personality than by offering some free YouTube videos to deliver, again, quality and value. Your viewers have the option to subscribe to your channel, and if you are consistent and decide YouTube works for you, this is a good way to build a following there as well. Ideas for promoting on YouTube include:

- Videos of you speaking or teaching about a topic in your area of expertise
- Screen-share video tutorials where you show your viewers how to do something online
- Meditations narrated by you with inspiring scenery and royalty-free music in the background
- A book trailer that links to your book's sales page

The sky's the limit with YouTube, so get creative, and who knows, maybe your video will go viral and then in addition to growing your list of subscribers you can also make some money on your videos. Yes, YouTube will begin to pay you if your video gets enough hits, and you can also monetize your videos with ads if you so choose.

Start a Podcast

One way to build a following is by starting your own podcast. Later when we discuss marketing your book, we will go over booking podcast interviews, but in this case, I am referring to creating your own podcast that you host, based on a topic in your area of expertise. This is not only a good way to build your tribe, but a podcast will lend credibility, and over time as you interview high-profile professionals in your field, it will build your circle of connections. Think about it, if you interview a few high-profile people on your podcast, and they are marketing the interview to their own list, you have the opportunity to convert your guest's list to new listeners, expanding your audience and *your* platform.

There's a small investment to start your own podcast, but you can do it affordably at first and then upgrade your equipment as your show grows in popularity. You'll need a quality microphone, some audio editing software, artwork for your cover art, perhaps a custom intro and outro, and a hosting account. You don't need much to get started, and you can have your podcast up and running in no time. Once you record and host your shows, you'll want to share them on podcast directories. The neat thing about a podcast is that they don't have to be the exact same amount of time each day as in a radio show. You could have a 30-minute podcast one day and then a 90-minute show the next, but I would caution you to aim for consistency and deliver a high-quality show, with interesting and fresh content for your listeners. Don't sell them short or get lazy; if you make the commitment to start a podcast, see it through. If you have a daily or weekly podcast, be sure your show is available at your scheduled time, as promised.

JB Glossinger is a great example of podcasting done right. He is known in his industry as the Morning Coach, delivering inspirational messages on personal development, but he not only has a podcast, MorningCoach®, that delivers 15-minute messages to start each day, he also has a membership site, www. morningcoach.com, where he houses his recordings and offers bonuses for membership, and his tribe pays a monthly fee to belong to his site. Genius! He even struck a deal with Hay House, and upon publication of his book, *The Sacred 6*, he was offered his own radio show on Hay House Radio, The Lifestyle Entrepreneur. Now there's an authorpreneur on fire!

Starting a podcast takes time, and you shouldn't make the commitment unless you are 100% certain you are going to give it the attention it deserves and follow through on that commitment.

If you announce that you are going to air your podcast five days a week, then you'd better be sure you can live up to your commitment and honor your word. I would suggest starting out slowly, with one or two shows per week, and adding more over time if that is your goal.

Brand Consistency

You'll want to ensure your branding is consistent across all platforms. It's a good idea to hire a designer to create your website design, logo, business cards, and coordinating social media banners so everything matches and looks professional. For example, if your colors are black and gold on your website, you don't want purple and green on your Twitter header. It's also a good idea to schedule a photo shoot and use that series of photos across all platforms. Your "About" page on your website might include your headshot, and this would also make a nice photo for your Facebook profile picture. If not the same one, then one in a different pose but from the same shoot. This will keep your branding consistent and help you to become easily recognizable online.

Some of these options may not be feasible in the beginning while you are building your empire. For those of you who are looking to DIY in the beginning, free online software such as Canva or PicMonkey may be great tools for you to develop your banners, logos, email headers and social media graphics. As your business grows and you start to bring in income, roll that income back into your business and upgrade your design slowly. You aren't expected to do it all at once. As long as you are upgrading when you can and consistently rolling funds back into your business, you will have an empire you can be proud of in no time.

Tying it All Together

So now you have your website, you have your list, and you have two to three social media accounts that you are consistently active on while building your tribe. How can you use these online tools to drive traffic to your list?

- Create social media graphics
- Add your handle or website to your social media graphics and headers
- Engage your audience and ask questions to prompt interaction
- Show up where your avatar is hanging out and offer value to showcase your expertise
- Fill out the description on your social media pages and add a link to your website, your other social media profiles, Facebook group, mailing list, etc.
- Utilize your blog to write articles relevant to your area of expertise and share those articles via social media
- Consider using paid advertising or promoted posts to get in front of more viewers and to build your presence. You can drive traffic to your website or list through paid advertising as well
- Research the ins and outs of your preferred social media platforms and use them to your advantage
- Consistently add relevant articles to your blog with the use of keywords to assist in SEO

CHAPTER FIVE

Growing Your List

You'll need to nurture and grow your list, because along with your book and platform, it is an important level of focus in building your business. Ideally, you should begin building your list long before your book is published. What do I mean by list? This includes your subscribers, your tribe, those most interested in what you have to offer. Most likely they've filled out a form on your website or through an opt-in because they want something you have to offer. This is your chance to convert them to clients. Don't let them slip away!

Opt-ins and Lead Magnets

How do you build your list? First and foremost, if you have a website, you need to have a way to collect email addresses as discussed in Chapter Four. But it's often not enough for us to add a form to our website asking our visitors to sign up for our newsletter or, as some do, even blatantly add, "Join my mailing list here." You will have greater success if you have an opt-in form with a lead magnet to entice them. You are probably thinking, what is a lead magnet? A lead magnet can be anything from a free eBook, a one-page PDF report, a checklist, your list of favorite productivity tools, an MP3 download—basically anything of value you can give away for free in exchange for an email address. Bribery? Maybe, but if you are giving away something of value, no need to feel bad about your intentions. Some examples of lead magnets that have worked well for me are my Top 20 Tools for Building an Author Empire, Book-Writing Planner, or my Book Launch and Marketing Checklist. They are all simple PDF downloads delivered through an auto-responder once someone opts-in to my list. None of them took me long to create and all have been invaluable in adding aspiring authors and writers to my list—my target audience.

This doesn't have to be complicated. One of my best con-verting lead magnets is only two pages! If you hop over to www.shandatrofe.com you'll find the opt-in: **My Top 20 Tools for Building an Author Empire.** I simply picked out the tools that work best for me, included a graphic and brief summary for each one, and converted the file to a PDF from Canva. I could have easily done this through Word as well if I wanted to keep it sim-ple. The reason this opt-in works so well for my target audience is because at this point I am targeting aspiring authorpreneurs. When you see someone doing something that is working well for them in their business, don't you want to know how they do it? I'm happy to share the tools I've used to build my empire, and it's a valuable resource for my tribe because I'm taking the guesswork out of it for them. If you'd like to see how an opt-in works and is delivered, go ahead and sign up for my free report. You can unsubscribe afterward if you don't care to be on my list. No hard feelings.

Once you know who your target audience is, think of what tools or information you could offer them that gives a taste of your style, delivers value, and will entice them to enter their information in exchange for the offer. To deliver your offer, you can set up a follow-up series through your email management system, or on the thank you page of an opt-in funnel. When someone subscribes to my list, I have a follow-up series in place to instantly deliver their first email. That first email welcomes them, thanks them, and then delivers their freebie, as promised. To take this one step further you can set up a few more emails in your follow-up series that are scheduled to be delivered a few days apart. Each email can offer a bit of your backstory or something of value, since your subscriber will need to trust you before they will buy. At the end of your series, you'll deliver your offer to either work with you or purchase one of your products or programs. And that's a simple funnel to get you started.

For now, work on how to get your target audience on your list by creating your lead magnet, and then later when you have more products you can develop a good funnel and add to your email sequence.

Another tool you can use to deliver your lead magnet is my go-to fave for all things online marketing: ClickFunnels. I use it to create my opt-ins, sales pages, create my upsell and thank you pages, host membership areas and courses, and it's also how I collect payment as it integrates seamlessly with my Stripe account. It can also deliver my lead magnets, because it integrates with my list, or you can use their email management service and then you don't need to worry about list integration. They are a one-stop-shop for all your online marketing needs, and they offer free webinars, training videos, and have quality customer support so you can learn how to use their platform effectively. Once you do, you will be hooked. There is a monthly fee for the service, so this may be something you add over time, but for me it's become a staple in my toolbox and I couldn't have scaled my business to six-figures without it. Or perhaps I could have, but it would have taken much longer! Other similar products that are quite popular are LeadPages, Kajabi, and SamCart. I've used all three, and have found that ClickFunnels will save you time and energy by eliminating extra steps needed to connect your funnel and make it function and convert. You can get a two-week free trial of ClickFunnels here through my affiliate link.

Webinars

Webinars are one of the highest converting tools you can use to drive traffic to your book or program while building your list. Usually webinars will offer valuable information, followed by a paid offer at the end. I jump on webinars all the time, even though I know at the end I am going to be encouraged to buy something, because a good webinar will deliver just the right amount of valuable information and give you a taste of the presenter's personality and teaching style, so you know by the end if you want to invest in their product or program.

If you decide to host a webinar, be sure you are delivering quality content, and consider adding a fraction of what they would learn from your course or product. Your presentation will usually be conducted as a screen share of your computer screen, showcasing slides with bullet points as you talk during the presentation, with you stopping to engage every so often to ask your participants to answer a question in the comments area to invoke interaction. At the end you can present your offer and those who have stayed with you throughout the entire 45-90 minutes are likely to buy. Now, there are some who will jump on your webinar just to learn your tip or trick, and then leave, without any intention of buying from you or purchasing from you, and that's OK. Let them go. They are not your tribe.

Once you nail a presentation, you can convert it to an auto-webinar that can be watched on demand. This is ideal so that you can make sales around the clock.

How does a webinar lead to book sales, you may ask? I don't know about you, but when I invest in a product or program from anyone, and they mention they are the author of a book on the subject, I usually head over to Amazon to download or buy the book just to be sure I want to invest in them further. The book is a low cost investment, and a great way to get an idea of what the person has to offer. Plus, webinars will grow your list rapidly, and the more people you have on your list, the more people to whom you can market your book. If you have a link to your book in the signature of your email, then each time you mail out to your list they will see that. Just because you aren't necessarily hosting a webinar with the intention of promoting your book at the end doesn't mean they won't find it inadvertently.

But the sole purpose of your webinar will not be to gain book sales. Usually you will do webinars to grow your list, and pitch a program or service at the end, such as an online course, member-ship site, or a high ticket program. However, it's important to deliver plenty of value during your presentation.

A good rule of thumb is to under-promise and then over-deliver. You want someone to walk away from your webinar having learned a new tool or trick they can implement in their life or business, without having to buy anything at all. But of course, to learn more or to continue to work with you further, they will have the option of taking your offer at the end. Don't sell your viewers short. In the long run, they will trust you more and become your devoted tribe if you over deliver on your promise and offer incredible value.

Joint Ventures

You have given it your best effort, but you can only do so much. Once you've brainstormed all the ways you can think of to build your list, it's time to enlist the help of others, particularly those with a large list who can benefit you, and vice versa. So how do you do that? Through joint ventures, more commonly known as JV's. This is where you combine forces with someone else to market each other's products to each other's list, in turn expanding your reach, gaining a new audience, and growing your subscribers. Why would you want to market someone else's product to your list? Well, for one, it's an even exchange, and two, you wouldn't if you didn't believe in the product or if the person was in direct competition with you. Finding the *right* JV partners where you both complement each other but are not in direct competition is the key. If you find someone with a nice-size list you may ask them to market your book, product or service to their list in exchange for an affiliate commission, or you could simply offer the same to them in exchange, with the assumption that you have a decent-size list as well and can offer them value. As your business starts to grow, you may find that JV partners will begin to seek *you* out. When that happens, you'll know you are doing something right!

Keep an open mind when choosing JVs to partner with, but use your best judgment as well. If it doesn't feel right, don't do it. You should have good chemistry with your JV partners and a mutual respect for one another.

An example of a JV partnership that works well in my business is when a colleague, who's usually a coach, invites me into her membership or group coaching program as a guest speaker to teach a workshop on book-writing or self-publishing. At the end, I make the audience an offer to work with me further, and if they accept, I offer my JV partner a percentage of the sales. It's a win-win for both of us because it allows me to get in front of a new audience for free, and it benefits my JV partner since my presentation offers value for her clients and students, and she gets to earn some additional income as well.

Paid Advertising

Once you have your lead magnet created and set up on your website to add visitors to your list, another option is to promote your lead magnet on social media with paid advertising. It's true what I said about a lean startup, but as your business grows, this is a great way to consistently add to your list. Plus, since Facebook, Instagram, and YouTube advertising allows you to get highly targeted, you can ensure your advertisement is shown to your ideal audience, those who will be interested in what you have to offer.

For example, I usually launch my Author Success Academy in the first quarter of the year, so beginning in January I run several sponsored ads on Facebook during my launch phase. My PDF Book-Writing Planner is the perfect lead magnet for this, especially since it's a time of year when aspiring authors typically set out to crush their goals and are full of motivation.

Once someone clicks on one of my ads, they are redirected to an opt-in form where they can enter their name and email address in exchange for my Book-Writing Planner, and are added to my list and follow-up email series. Then, they are immediately sent my free PDF download. Over the course of two weeks, they'll receive the rest of my follow-up series of emails. At the end of the series, after they've heard from me several times, the final email introduces my upcoming Academy (my high-end offer) and many of my target audience usually ends up enrolling.

Getting Facebook advertising right is a science and you can purchase programs to help you create high-converting Facebook ads if you have the time and energy to invest in the training. Since Facebook is constantly changing their algorithm, it's important to find the latest information from someone who is actively updating their content to stay relevant.

If you are going to dabble in paid advertising, it's a good idea to start with a low budget on a few smaller ads to test what works and what doesn't. Once you find the ad that is converting best, then you can up the ante. As your business grows, your budget will grow as well, and you can place more ads on a larger scale.

You are probably thinking, wouldn't it have been easier if I had just placed a Facebook ad for my course and had it linked to the sales page? The simple answer is NO. And I know this to be true because when I first got started, that is what I did. It simply doesn't convert as well. I may have gained one or two students that way, but creating opt-ins, lead magnets and a follow-up series delivered through email autoresponders will be crucial to your success. Yes, it is time consuming, but definitely worth it. Remember, you need to gain a prospect's trust before they will invest in you, so you need to set up a funnel via your follow-up series/autoresponders and deliver valuable content before you ask for the sale or present your high-end offer.

Guest Blogging

There are some who just don't resonate with Facebook, and don't believe in spending money on targeted Facebook ads to build a list. If you fall into that camp, that's OK; it's not mandatory to use Facebook or pay for advertising at all. There are many ways to build your list for free, such as guest blogging.

A simple Google search for popular blogs within your niche should return some quality leads. In the search bar, use the keywords related to your topic and include the word "blog" at the end. Search for respected bloggers with a large audience and become active on their blog by commenting often. Be sure your comments are professional and constructive, never negative or unprofessional. Contact the blog administrator from their contact page. Write an email informing him/her that you have been following their blog (add some praise for their work to back up your claim), and you have something of value to add and can offer a positive contribution as a guest blogger. It's also helpful to pitch your article idea in that email and be sure to write about a topic within your selected niche. Usually when you are a guest blogger the administrator will allow you to include your title, bio (this is where that short 50-word bio we talked about will come in handy), the title of your book, your website and contact information. When done right, guest blogging can grow your list astronomically, and is a great way to showcase your writing and position yourself as an expert in your field.

Become a Regular Contributor

You can share your expertise regularly on a variety of platforms that you don't have to host yourself as you would with your blog. An easy way to do this is by becoming a regular contributor for larger online publications such as Medium, Entrepreneur, Addicted2Success, or Success Magazine–just to name a few. The perk of these types of platforms is that they have their own audiences, which usually include a large list of subscribers–sometimes in the millions–so it's a great way to showcase your expertise and attract new readers and potential clients.

Live Video Broadcasting

Live video broadcasting has exploded in popularity. Through platforms such as Facebook, Instagram, and YouTube, you can now post live videos to an audience who is watching and engaging while you are on air. This allows you to reach viewers all over the world from a mobile handheld device. You can air live Facebook videos, which is an effective tool for those who wish to be known for delivering valuable information within your niche. There are many ways you can use live video broadcasting for business; but for now I will tell you the gist of it: scope out your target audience and deliver cutting-edge information and valuable tips relevant to your business or area of expertise. This will help you build a following of subscribers who are eager to jump on your broadcast when they see the notification that you are live. Always be offering value. Over deliver. Be good to your tribe. This establishes trust and is also a good business practice, so later when you launch your book, online course or mentoring program, your followers will be familiar with your work, your teaching style, your personality, and hopefully are eagerly waiting to work with you.

At the end of your video broadcast, after you've delivered value, end with a call-to-action to join your list or visit your website. You may even use your live video broadcast to launch a product such as your book or a new product or service you are offering. Think of this as you would a webinar: give valuable free information, over deliver, and then make an offer at the end if they would like to learn more or continue to work with you. Keep in mind, your viewers don't want to be sold to each time you go live, just like your newsletter subscribers don't want to be sold to in each email they receive from you. The goal is to consistently offer valuable information, tips and resources for free, with offers for your products and services added sporadically or during your launch phases.

> **TIP:** Once you have a variety of products and services to offer, it's a good idea to create a marketing calendar for the year and schedule your launches as well as your JV promotions accordingly to ensure your list isn't constantly bombarded with "salesy" emails and offers to purchase. Those should be spread out and scheduled appropriately.

Host a Summit

Hosting a summit is a lot of work, but it's one of the fastest ways to build your list. The idea is that you find 20 or more experts in your field with 5,000 subscribers or more each, and ask them to be a part of your summit, where you record a twenty-minute interview with each of the experts. Once you have all the interviews recorded, each of the twenty experts promotes the summit to their list, which is free. However, the interested party has to opt-in to your list to gain access to the recorded interviews that you will release over a condensed time frame, usually five days, hence building your list by leveraging the lists of the twenty experts. The benefit for your chosen experts is that you will allow them to give away a freebie/lead magnet, and it can in turn grow their list as well and often allow them to add new clients. This is an advanced technique with many moving parts, and I don't recommend hosting one without the guidance of someone who has already done it.

With any of these list-building techniques, the key is to always deliver high-quality information for free, over delivering on your promise, all the while being mindful not to give it *all* away so that you'll gain a subscriber who wants more of what you have to offer. This means bite-size pieces of valuable free information that are a part of something larger you have to offer, such as your book, coaching program, membership site, online course, etc.

CHAPTER SIX

Let's Talk Publishing

Let's talk publishing, shall we? When it's time to publish your book, you'll have many options to choose from, and my goal is to educate you on those options so you can make the decision that's best for you. Although I own a self-publishing company, I am not going to tell you my way is the best, because my publishing model isn't a good fit for every author and I tell my clients that. My goal is to offer you an honest overview of your publishing options so you can make your own educated decision. I would encourage you to spend some time researching beyond what I teach in this book, and put some thought into it before making your final decision.

Traditional Publishing

The publishing industry has changed over the years. There was a time when traditional publishing was the only respectable option, but that didn't always mean success for the aspiring author. It used to be that in order to find representation by a publisher you would have to first find an agent to represent you and your book, and that was done through a querying process to determine if

77

the agent was interested in reading the book proposal you'd spent months to develop. If after twenty or thirty query letters you actually got a few agents asking to see your proposal, at that point you would deliver it to the agent and then wait with bated breath to learn if they were interested in representing you.

Let's say for the sake of this example, an agent did decide to take you on as a client; they then would shop your manuscript around to traditional publishers in exchange for a cut of the royalties. Now, this might be a good place to mention that the industry standard royalty from a traditional publisher is 10-15%, sometimes even as low as 5-8%, and that is after the distribution costs are considered. Yes, you might have received an advance from your traditional publishing house, but you won't see another cent from them until your advance is paid back through your royalty cut.

When a traditional publisher decides to represent you, they essentially buy the rights to your book, meaning they have complete creative control over your cover, title, structure of the book, overall design, which takes 18-24 months to produce on average, and they can even kill a project if they want. Some books never even make it to publication at all. That seems like a lot of time and work to invest in gambling with my book. Most authors spend years thinking about their book before they actually write it, and then put their heart and soul into the project once they do. What a shame to lose creative control over the publishing process and the rights to the book. I don't know about you but everything about that process seems exhausting. I'm tired just thinking about it!

It may sound like I am completely against traditional publishing, but I'm not. There are times when I tell even my own clients that they should pursue a traditional publishing model. If a client comes to me and tells me it's their life-long dream to be represented by one of the top publishing houses, I tell them to go for it. When it's a goal to meet a personal accomplishment, and having a certain publisher's name adorn the spine of the book, then who am I to stand in the way of an author's dream? And being picked up by a top publishing house can bring exposure and opportunity, so there are perks. But if the goal of the author is to get a book out in a reasonable amount of time so they can use it as a product for their business, retain the rights to the work and maintain creative control over the entire process, that's when I recommend they explore other options.

Here are some tips for pursuing a traditional publisher:

Consider whether you will need a literary agent. Some traditional publishing houses will not accept unsolicited queries. If you have a publisher in mind and through your research you've learned they do not accept unsolicited queries, you will find it helpful to engage a literary agent to represent you. This has its pros and cons. Yes, they can help you get your foot in the door with top publishing houses, but you are going to pay them a percentage to represent you. If you decide to seek out the help of a literary agent, find an agent that prefers to represent your genre. For example, you would not want to query a literary agent who has a strong interest in sci-fi for your personal memoir. Most agents will list their preferences on their website, and literary agents along with their contact information are listed in the latest copy of the *Writer's Market*. Be sure to study your preferred agent's query requirements and follow them to a tee. You might consider reading some related-subject books or taking a workshop on the art of querying before continuing.

Develop a strong book proposal. You can find many books and websites out there that will walk you through the layout of a book proposal. Be sure the information you are reading is up to date. You also want to be sure your proposal is free of grammatical errors, has proper punctuation, and is in the correct format. Keep in mind that each publisher may require different criteria. If you are not going to use an agent, it is best to seek out your desired publishers by thoroughly researching their specifications.

Be professional. Once you start sending out queries and proposals, make sure each communication with the contact person is conducted in a professional manner. Don't get too comfortable with your point of contact. Watch for punctuation, grammar, and always start and end each email with the proper greeting and closure. If you make an appointment to speak on the phone, be available at that time and prepared to answer questions about your project. It is important to stay in contact, follow up and meet deadlines.

Be persistent. If you are going to work at getting published by a traditional publisher, you are going to have to develop a thick skin. If you receive a rejection, don't let it get you down or cause you to lose faith in your gift or lose sight of your goal. It could just mean you weren't the right fit for that particular publisher and a better opportunity awaits you just around the corner.

Be prepared to hear several NOs before you hear one YES. Set realistic expectations and recognize that it is tough to break into the traditional publishing world. Above all, be persistent.

There are times when traditional publishing may be the right way to go, especially if you receive an offer by a respectable publisher such as Hay House, Random, or HarperCollins. You might do it for the recognition, you may do it for their reach, you might do it to build your list, you could just do it for the experience of it all and to say you are published by such-and-such publishing house.

Self-Publishing

Self-published books were once looked down upon, and rightfully so, if you think about it. The traditionally published authors who spent months querying agents, crafting book proposals, and waiting on pins and needles only to receive rejection letter after rejection letter until they finally found a publisher who was willing to represent their work, had little respect for the self-published author.

The eBook boom and print-on-demand publishing services haven't helped much, since now any old Joe can upload a manuscript to Amazon and call himself an author. The number of amateur books that began to flood Amazon was a joke to the traditionally published author, and for good reason.

Although self-publishing can be a lucrative and viable option when done right, some authors didn't take the process seriously and didn't realize there's an investment that comes with self-publishing to do it properly. Even though you can upload a book to a print-on-demand service and have it live on Amazon within days, sometimes even hours, that doesn't mean it's always the right way to go.

Personally, I respect the self-published author, especially when he or she has taken the time to scope out and hire professionals to ensure their book is published at the highest level of quality and doesn't scream DIY.

Not all self-published authors take the fast and easy route, and now it's become the norm to see professional-quality self-published books by indie authors. Self-published authors aren't the outcasts they once were, and it's a growing practice among writers. In fact, as of 2020, 1.7 million new books were self-published in the U.S. That's an increase of 264% within the past five years and makes up 43% of the total new books published[1].

Self-publishing may be a good option for you if you are willing to invest the time and money to do it right. This way, you retain the rights to your work and you have creative control over the entire project. And it can be done in a timely manner, instead of waiting 12-18 months as you would through a traditional publisher. Thus, this is an ideal option if you are creating a book for your business since you will retain more of the profits.

The book you create for your business is the ultimate extension of you and your work. It represents everything you have to offer, so if you decide to self-publish, be sure to invest the proper time and energy into writing and publishing the best book possible. Do not skim on the investment of professional design

---

[1] https://www.zippia.com/advice/us-book-industry-statistics/

services. When creating a book as the base of your empire, this isn't the time to be lean; it's a time to invest.

Costs you'll need to invest in to self-publish a high-quality book:

- ISBN
- Professional Editing
- Professional Cover Design
- Custom Interior Design
- Formatted Digital Edition (eBook)
- Launch to Bestseller
- Advertising
- Marketing Graphics
- Proofreading

You can easily spend thousands to self-publish, launch and market your book, if you give it your best effort and do it properly so it has the high-quality of a traditionally published book. Some feel if they are going to spend the money to self-publish, they might as well partner with a company or service who already has all the necessary quality connections and design professionals on staff, as defined in the next two sections.

Hybrid/Independent Publishers

Hybrid publishers bridge the gap between self-publishing and traditional publishing by offering full packages that include editing, design services, and the launch, but they typically publish your book through their own publishing imprint and pay you a percentage of the royalties, while they retain a percentage as well. Royalty splits with an independent publisher can range anywhere from 25-80%, much higher than the 10-15% industry standard you'd receive from a traditional publisher.

You're probably thinking, *That sounds great! What's the catch?* Well, you're essentially self-publishing but you aren't retaining all of your net royalties as you would if you published your book through your own publishing account and imprint. This is why we stopped offering Hybrid publishing via Transcendent Publishing back in 2018. I realized we could still offer our clients the same design services and done-for-you self-publishing packages, but I could instead have them set up their own publishing account, grant us temporary access, and we upload the files, add the metadata, and set up everything on their behalf, allowing them to retain 100% of their net royalties. This offers our authors more control of their books post-publication, and they don't have to wait for a royalty check from us as they now get paid out directly from the distributor.

I'll go over our publishing model more in the next section, but if you're still interested in working with a Hybrid/Independent Publisher, I've added a list of questions I recommend you ask if you decide to pursue this model. If it is an honest company that does business with integrity, they should be able to answer each of these questions, in detail, in a timely manner. These aspects of the agreement should be decided upfront and outlined in your contract before production begins. Be sure there are no hidden costs you might incur at a later date.

- What is your average publishing turnaround time?
- How much say do I have in cover design and what is your process?
- How many changes to my cover proof can I make?

- Do you offer professional editing services? If so, how many rounds of editing do I receive?
- Is there an extra fee for that service?
- What is the cost of each publishing package?
- What is included in each package?
- What would be considered an add-on or upgrade?
- Does that include illustrations or color interior, if requested?
- What book styles and binding types are available?
- Will I incur costs after production begins, in addition to the cost of my package?
- What would cause any additional fees to be incurred after production begins?
- Will I receive a PDF proof prior to publication?
- If so, will I be allowed to make changes at that time? How many?
- Will I sign off on the proof prior to publication?
- Upon publication, do you assist with marketing efforts?
- What is my royalty percentage of print sales?
- What is my royalty percentage of digital sales?
- What will be my wholesale cost per book?
- Do you have an order minimum for wholesale orders?
- Do I receive a discount on bulk orders?
- Will my publishing package include an eBook as well as print?
- Will my book be softcover or hardcover, or both?
- Does my package include the audiobook?

- Do you assist with marketing efforts, post publication? How so?

- Does your company have a mission statement so I can be sure we are a good fit for one another?

Assisted Publishing with Complete Self-Publishing Packages

Due to the rise of indie authors and the popularity of self-publishing, companies offering assisted self-publishing packages and services are growing in popularity, and author-funded publishing programs are becoming more and more common. This is the model my company has been using to serve our authors for the past four years since we switched from Hybrid publishing. Typically, it's a one-stop-shop for all of your publishing needs such as coaching, editing, cover and interior design, and the launch to bestseller, but the author still maintains creative control over the project and retains the rights to the book plus 100% of their net royalties since we upload the files directly to your own publishing account on your behalf.

Instead of an author looking everywhere for a cover designer, and then a quality editor, and a book formatter, a project manager, and marketing resources, now the author can partner with one company who has all the seasoned professionals on staff to ensure the book is high-quality and the best it can be prior to publication. However, instead of splitting the royalties with a hybrid publisher, authors are instead published through their own publishing account directly with their distributor(s) such as Kindle Direct Publishing (KDP), IngramSpark, and Barnes and Noble Press. There are more to choose from which you should research, but those are the three I prefer for my clients.

With this model you will purchase a self-publishing package and pay for the services upfront (or on a payment plan, depending on the company), but in exchange for that you'll have a team of experts, design professionals and a project manager working with you on the creation and production of your project throughout the entire process. This is money you would have spent on self-publishing anyway if you went that route, so many authors see the value in purchasing a done-for-you package and funding the project to ensure the book is created to the highest of standards.

What You Need to Know

A word of caution: There are some unethical predators in the publishing industry, and there are some who are only after the almighty buck and don't conduct business with integrity, such as vanity presses which offer poor quality and often fail to deliver on their promise. I know this firsthand, and it was my own experience with one of these publishers that in 2012 led me to start my own publishing company.

Over the years I have heard horror stories from many authors, from all publishing models. I've heard from the traditionally published author who was mortified after she received the final product only to find her cover and title were changed. She had to do the majority of marketing for the book, despite being traditionally published, and after the publisher takes their cut when each book sells, she only makes approximately $1 per book. You'd have to have a lot of sales to make any amount of money as an author at $1 per book! Traditional publishers seldom take you by the hand and fund book tours, signings, and speaking engagements. Although it still happens for the bigger, well-known authors, it's typically unheard of for a first-time author.

I've also heard from the self-published author who spent time and money seeking the best cover designer, editor, and formatter, to self-publish his book through KDP and have it available on Amazon. He was proud of his book and had spent hundreds, maybe even thousands on its production. He went to his local Barnes and Noble and was able to get a meeting with the book buyer for the store. He was stoked about the meeting, only to have the wind let out of his sails. It wasn't due to the lack of a good product that his book got rejected by the bookstore; it was because it was published solely through KDP, and books that are published only by KDP are not likely to be picked up by larger bookstores because they are not in the book returnability program. This is something most self-published authors don't know. In order for a larger bookstore to carry your book, they want to know they can return it in the event it doesn't sell. The problem? Bookstores can't return books to KDP, making it nearly impossible to get the book into stores. For this particular self-published author, his book was available on Amazon and he could buy copies as needed from the printer, but his chances of adorning the shelves of bookstores across America were shot.

If your goal is to get your book into bookstores, libraries, or universities, and attain global distribution, you'll want to ensure your book is distributed through IngramSpark as well, so it's available via global distribution channels, registered with books-in-print, and has a book buyback plan.

If you'd like a step-by-step guide on how to self-publish, along with a breakdown of each of your options, I cover the full process in great detail in my book, *Self-Publishing Success.*

The decision to write and publish a book is one that should not be taken lightly. It is an extension of you and your business.

You'll want to take the time necessary to do your research and find the publishing option that is right for you and your project. This is your baby, after all, and it should be nurtured and birthed when the timing is right and you've thoroughly examined all of your options. This includes having overseen the production of the book to completion, developed a book launch strategy and plan of action, and being ready to put your book out into the world—a book you are proud of and around which you can build a business.

All publishing options have their pros and cons. Here's a table to help you decide which publishing option is right for you:

	Production & Design Decisions	Royalty (after costs)	Rights	Marketing
Traditional Publishing	Publisher	8-15%	Publisher	Both, but primarily Author
Hybrid/ Independent Publisher	Publisher w/ the Author's input	25-80%	Author	Primarily Author; sometimes w/ light assistance from Publisher
Self- Publishing	Author, w/ the project manager's input (optional)	100%	Author	Author

Digital (eBook) Publishing

The days are long gone when an author would only publish a book in print. Nowadays, almost all new print editions are accompanied by a digital edition. I mention this so you can understand why your book also needs to be in a digital format, even if it's not *your* preferred method of reading books.

E-books sold 191 million units in 2020, which was a sharp 12.6% increase over 2019[2]. If you don't have your book available as a digital download, you are missing out on valuable web sales from popular distributors such as Kindle, Nook, iBooks, Kobo, and more. Some may argue that digital publishing is the only way to go, that eBooks are going to kill print publishing so there's no sense in publishing your book in print. As an author and publisher, I disagree. Sure, there are times when I see value in creating eBooks alone. I have some clients who *only* publish digitally and do quite well for themselves (mostly fiction authors). One of my most popular online courses is eBook Publishing Made Easy: Write & Publish Kindle eBooks for Profits, so believe me when I tell you, I love digital publishing, it was my first love in this publishing industry, after all. But I don't agree that it's the only way. You need your book in print as well if you are utilizing it for business, in my opinion.

Don't get me wrong, there are times when it's acceptable to only have a digital book available. Case in point, I had an eBook that I wrote primarily to funnel readers from Amazon to one of my online courses. When Periscope grew in popularity (yes, I'm dating myself here), I devoured all the info on it I could find and became obsessed with how Periscope worked and what the top

---

[2] https://www.zippia.com/advice/us-book-industry-statistics/

broadcasters were doing successfully. Next, I developed an online course, Periscope Your Business: Live Video Broadcasting for Profits, one of the very first online courses on Periscope, and to drive traffic to that course I created a companion eBook with the same title: *Periscope Your Biz.* I published the eBook on Amazon through KDP and set the price low to attract more readers. I wasn't trying to get rich off my .99 cent Periscope eBook, what I was doing instead was driving traffic to my course, which I linked at the end of the book through a strong call-to-action page. The idea was if they found value in the book (and I gave just enough information to offer value without giving it all away) and they wanted to learn more, then my Periscope course was just what they needed. In situations like that I believe it's fine to only publish in digital format. It was a 50-page book, after all, so why would I publish in print? But this was a funneling technique, not the core product for my business as your book will be, so in your case, you'll want to ensure your book is published in both print and digital formats.

The moral of the story is there are times when it's a lucrative option to create some shorter how-to eBooks on a subtopic in your niche, or to create a series of short eBooks. But for your signature book, the one we are creating here as the foundation of your empire, you'll want it in print as well as digital. Don't do one without the other. For the book representing your business, you'll want both.

Now, that's not to say that after your book is published you won't have smaller spin-off eBooks on various sub-topics discussed in your book; you could create a whole series of how-to eBooks that never make it to print. This is where eBooks as companion products come in handy. I'll give you an example: This very book you are reading was once the foundation of my business, back in 2016 when I published its first edition. All the programs I developed after the publication of this book were based on the topic of the book and the subtopics discussed within. I could have, if I'd wanted to, created a series of eBooks that break down the teachings from this book into smaller bites. Each eBook would not only link to the others in the back, but it would also link to this book and my online programs and services.

The first page sells this book. The last page sells your next book.

—Mickey Spillane

Additionally, Amazon will allow you to create a series page to house all of the books in your series, and when they are connected in this way, Amazon will advertise each book in the series on every book's product page–a great way to get your readers to purchase every book in the series.

Do you see how eBooks can be a valuable tool in your empire? Not only will you want to be sure to publish your flagship book in a digital format as well as print, but you can also look at ways to break down your topic into subtopics and create smaller eBooks of 50-100 pages to create a series and funnel readers into your main book and high-end programs.

Not to mention, if your eBook is priced between $2.99 and $9.99 Amazon will pay you a 70% royalty on the sale. Outside those brackets you'll receive a 35% royalty. Not bad if you create a series of books that really takes off or you jump on a hot topic as I did when Periscope was launched. Although my goal for that eBook was more to direct readers to my online course, since it was a hot topic and there were very few books on the market about Periscope at the time of publication, I also made quite a bit of money off that little eBook. Score!

Research Your Options

No matter which publishing option you choose, the choice is yours, so don't let others dictate what you should or should not do with your project. Only you will know what's best for you and your book, so take some time to research not only your publishing options, but also the publishers or publishing services/programs you are interested in. Don't be afraid to ask questions, as many as you need, to be sure you are making the right decision. Publishing your book is not a decision you should take lightly. Dig in, learn the ins and outs, ask questions, and read, read, read. If you decide to go the traditional route, pick up the latest edition of Writer's Digest's *Writer's Market* for a list of publishers and agents. Be sure to research each of their guidelines before querying them, as they all vary.

But, as I've mentioned before, there usually isn't much money to be made from your book alone, unless of course you hit it big like J.K. Rowling or the James Pattersons of the world who would beg to differ, but their experience will likely be different. Chances are you will make more from your books if you self-publish or publish through an independent publisher, because your royalty split will be higher, you won't need a middleman (agent), and you are going to be marketing your book anyway. If you work hard at self-promotion, building your list, online marketing, and get out and do speaking engagements, workshops and live events, you can sell your book at each stop and keep the profits of any books sold by your own efforts. You can buy your books from your publisher or printer at the wholesale rate and resell them at the retail rate, and that can be lucrative, *if* you have a successful event or online presence, have a powerful message, and are in front of the right audience.

All of those pieces will factor into your success as an author. It's not enough just to write and publish a book and then sit back and wait for the money to roll in. I'm sorry, but it doesn't work that way. Being an author is work. It's an investment of not only money but time. And if you are willing to put in the work, you can find success, but to do so you'll need to be actively marketing your book, and putting yourself out there both in person and online.

The Moral of the Story

When you start researching publishing options for your book, let's say for argument's sake you do get a traditional publisher to show interest in your proposal, do you know what they are going to want to know first and foremost? What's your author platform, how big is your list, how many times have you been on television or radio, how many speaking engagements have you done? And let me tell you, it's not easy to build your list and it certainly takes time. A good-size list in a traditional publisher's eyes is 100,000+ people. That's a lot! How do you get that many people on your list?

First and foremost, you start today. Do not wait until your book is published, do not wait until you start writing even–start the second you decide you are going to have a book, product, or service to market.

Secondly, put yourself out there. Establish yourself as the expert in your field, even before your book is published. You need to be everywhere. Every speaking engagement, every interview, every networking event. Volunteer your time in exchange for your list building. Do free appearances; host free workshops. Later, when you have a large platform you might get lucky enough to be paid to speak, but not when you are building your list. When you are building, you are going to be doing things for free, and there are some people who even pay a lot of money to speak at certain events, and they do it because they know they will get a return on their investment. Their message will speak to a few people in the audience and they will walk away with a few more members of their tribe.

It takes time and it takes effort. I'm not telling you it will be easy, I'm telling you to start now and don't waste another second.

CHAPTER SEVEN

Promoting Your Book

Authors often ask me when is the best time to start promoting their book. My answer is simple: *at least* six months prior to publication. You want to start building a buzz around your book launch long before your book is published. You can do this many ways, through communicating updates and excerpts through your newsletter, your blog, teaser graphics on your website and social media. You can also do pre-sale activities leading up to publication day.

But what about when your book is finally published, then what? If you think the hard work is over, I have news for you, there is still much to be done. Some authors launch a book and actively market it for six months, ultimately abandoning their efforts. The problem with that is, often you are quitting right before your breakthrough. If you are going to make the commitment to write and publish a book, why would you quit so soon? The reality is you should make a commitment to actively market your book for as long as it's available for purchase. If you want your book to be a success, if you want to grow your list, if you want to build your empire, you have to make an active effort in marketing.

Don't think your publisher, if you have one, is going to do all the work for you. The sad reality is, most publishers expect *you* to front marketing efforts, and even if you've partnered with a publisher who has agreed to market with you, you are still responsible for actively marketing your book. It is the foundation of *your* business, and you should never get complacent or lazy with it. Now that we've got that settled, let's talk marketing strategies.

> **You can write the most wonderful book in the world. But if people don't know about your book they won't know to buy it.**
>
> **—Madi Preda**

Media Kit

A press/media kit can be useful when contacting people in the media for publicity, but not just for journalists, it may also be requested by bloggers, reviewers, interviewers, retailers, and anyone who might take an interest in your book. It will often contain all the information they need such as your author bio and contact information, your book's press release, and specific information about your book, including a sample Q&A for interviewers, testimonials and editorial reviews. If you are being interviewed or are seeking a write-up about you or your book, this will be extremely helpful to the interviewer or journalist when compiling research on you. You can add this as a page on your website, but it's also a good idea to have this available as a PDF to easily email upon request.

Blogging

Although it can be time consuming, and it's not as popular as it once was, blogging is still a great way to drive traffic to your website through SEO, and is a popular tool to use during any launch phase for a book or product. The people who opt-in to your list during concentrated efforts are people you can later target for your offer, so during a book launch, this would be a valuable period to invest time in blogging. To do so, you want to offer worthwhile information in your area of expertise, relevant to your book.

During the launch phase it's a good idea to create a blogging schedule and stick to it. If you feel it may be hard for you to stick to it, write each article in advance and schedule them to post at a certain date and time. Every two or three days, perhaps. Then, each time you publish a new article on your blog, share it via social media as well. Share links to the articles on Facebook, Twitter, Pinterest and LinkedIn, and any other social media outlets of choice. You may even promote the post through paid advertising to get the articles more traction during your launch phase, since promoted posts will be seen dependent upon the parameters you set.

At the time of writing this book, video is currently all the rage. If you're like me, your first inclination may be to shy away from video, but I urge you to break out of your comfort zone and try it.

> **Move out of your comfort zone. You can only grow if you are willing to feel awkward and uncomfortable when you try something new.**
> **—Brian Tracy**

Vlogging

Video blogging, or vlogging, has grown in popularity and for good reason: your tribe wants to see you! You may think: What if

I screw up? What if I make mistakes and lose my followers? If so, they weren't your true tribe to begin with. Your tribe wants to see you, and all your imperfections, too. Now I'm not saying that if you have a major fumble you shouldn't erase and re-record, but let them see YOU. They want to know that you are human too, that you are a real person just like them. Someone who makes mistakes from time to time. Plus, your viewers usually love getting an inside glimpse into your world—a behind-the-scenes look at your life, your office, inside your home, or wherever you are recording. This helps your tribe connect with you, it builds trust and loyalty, so don't shut them out. Give it a try, over time the fear of the camera will subside and before long you will be a natural.

You don't need any fancy equipment to get started; most videos can be made from a webcam or smartphone. Just be mindful of your backdrop, you'll want to create a setting that looks professional, and be sure there isn't an echo on the video. You can easily clean up audio from your video with programs like Audacity, or you can find someone on Fiverr.com to do it for you (if you are not familiar with Fiverr.com, check it out! Find freelancers for hire starting at only $5). If you decide you like video and want to upgrade your equipment, you can always invest in an affordable home studio with the proper lighting and recording equipment, but to get started, a webcam or smartphone should suffice.

Guest Blogging/Posting

In a previous chapter, I mentioned guest blogging for building your list, but you can also use it to promote your book. In this case, you wouldn't approach someone to allow you to write a guest post about your book, you'd want to promote it inadvertently. You would find a sub-topic related to your book, and write the blog post about that, then at the end of your post or in your bio, you would mention that you are the author of a book (include the title) on the topic and offer a link to find out more.

> **Tip:** To find popular blogs in your niche, check out BuzzSumo. It's an online resource (try out their 30-day free trial) and do a search for blogs centered on your topic or search using keyword(s). It will return the results of the most trending online content related to your search.

Here's a tip I learned from Mariah Coz, Creator of *Launch Your Signature Course*. Follow a blog that's relevant to your topic or area of expertise. When the blogger offers a suggestion or tool, implement that tool and track and record your progress. Measure the results and then email the blogger and share your results with them. Ask if they would like to feature you as a case study. Usually, if a blogger finds out that you have tried one of their suggestions and met with success, they will be happy to feature you on their blog, especially if you've kept good records and your results have proven their claims. As with guest blogging, the blogger will usually allow you to add your bio and contact info.

Reviews

One of the most important aspects besides your sales in terms of book ranking is reviews. It's important to get reviews on your book upon publication, because let's face it, people usually read reviews before they'll invest in a product, and a book without any reviews does not seem as credible. Getting reviews can be tricky, because it's considered unethical to pay for reviews, in fact it's against Amazon's Terms of Service, and it's also against their policy to have friends and family review your book; they will often remove reviews if they find a link between accounts. I personally recommend asking bloggers, known reviewers, and colleagues to read and review my books, and always ask for an honest review as it's also considered unethical to ask for a positive review.

You can easily find a list of Amazon's top reviewers by simply Googling "Amazon's Top Reviewers," and you can reach out and let them know about your book (briefly) and ask if they would be interested in reviewing it. Pubby and NetGalley have programs you can join and ask their members to review your book. Another option is to compile a book launch team and offer them an ARC (Advanced Reader Copy) in exchange for a review. Whenever you ask for reviews, it's important to be positive and professional, and know that getting a negative review will sometimes happen, but *please* don't lash out at the reviewer. You asked for an honest review, after all, and that's part of the turf. You'll need to develop a thick skin when it comes to reviews, because you won't be everyone's cup of tea. Try to set your ego aside and learn what you can from the review so you can use the feedback for what to do or not to do in the future. Although we hope that someone would just contact us directly to deliver less than stellar feedback about our hard work, that's not always the case. Shake it off and learn what you can from the review and apply it to your next edition or the next book in your series.

As an author you will sometimes receive emails from readers letting you know how much they enjoyed your book and thanking you. Those are the people you want to ask for a review. Take the time to reply and thank them for their kind words. Ask if they would consider taking a moment to leave a review for your book. If they took time out of their day to email you, chances are they will take some additional time to craft a review, especially since their fav new author reached out to them!

Finally, take time to leave reviews for other authors and they will likely return the favor. That's one of the things I love most about my Author Success Academy. With each launch, members ask the other authors in the group if they'd like to join their book launch team. They all support each other's launches, so joining a group of authors and offering your support is a great place to start.

Interviews

Once your book is published you will want to be interviewed by as many television, radio, and podcast hosts as possible. Booking these interviews may be easier than one might think. I used to have an internet radio show, *Write from the Heart*, where I interviewed a different author each week. Let me tell you, as a former radio show host I was always open to authors reaching out to be on my show and I rarely turned them down as long as they had a high-quality book and a positive message to share. Being interviewed on radio shows or podcasts can translate to tons of exposure for your book.

To get started, peruse podcast directories and contact hosts with shows relevant to your topic. Tell the host you are a published author and expert on [insert subject], and ask if they would be interested in an interview. Be sure to send your bio, website URL, and pitch up to three compelling interview topics that would be of interest to their audience. You might even consider taking this one step further and start your own podcast to host!

> **Tip:** Check out MatchMaker.fm, a community of 35,000+ people with the goal of connecting podcasters with guests. It's free to get started and create a profile.

Don't stop there. You can even contact your local media to book radio shows and television interviews in your area. One of my clients and colleagues, Jodie Harvala, Creator of Spirit School, does this quite often. She has found that a local morning radio show in her hometown often welcomes her to be a return guest because they are always looking to promote locals and showcase their success. Sometimes all you have to do is ask, so it doesn't hurt to pick up the phone and make a few calls or send a few emails.

Speaking Engagements

What better way to get the word out about your book than by being a guest speaker at upcoming conferences and events within your niche? Let's say, for example, your book topic is health and wellness. Do an online search for upcoming wellness events in your area and contact the organizer to ask if they are in need of speakers. Be sure to mention that you are a published author as that tends to be a requirement for many venues. They might also allow you to rent a booth where you can sell your books before and after your speaking engagement, or they may even offer you one for free. Depending on the event and the size of your platform, you may have to pay to speak, but this is often well worth the publicity and exposure in the beginning. Over time, as your platform grows, you may find that you are offered paid speaking gigs, but don't get discouraged when you are starting out and there is a fee to take the stage.

> **TIP:** Nervous about public speaking? There are many ways to polish your public speaking skills and a search for a local Toastmasters group is a good start. By joining Toastmasters, you will start by speaking to a small

group who will offer constructive criticism before you ever set foot on stage. To find a group near you, visit www.toastmasters.org.

Nowadays, online events are more popular than ever, so don't discount being asked to speak in a summit, during a Zoom workshop, or as a guest speaker for an online retreat. Once you become a published author, you'll be amazed at the opportunities that will open up for you to share your expertise. Remember, the goal is not to talk solely about your book, per se, but rather to offer value on the main topic or a subtopic within your book, and mention that you are an author and your book title in your bio and when you are introduced by the host.

Networking Events

Get out there in the community and rub elbows with those who can benefit from working with you or reading your book. There are likely many Meetup groups near you related to your interests. You can do a simple search for local Meetups on www.meetup.com. There are also many book clubs and community events in every locale. Become active in these groups and network with a like-minded community. Can't find a Meetup group in your niche? Why not start your own?

Book Signings

Contact your local bookstores and notify them that you are a locally published author. Ask if they would be interested in hosting a book signing at their store. There is also a good chance they will agree to carry your book on their shelves, and getting into your local bookstore is always a great idea. You'll usually need to arrange a meeting with the store manager for this. Other places to consider are your library, literary festivals, trade shows, churches, schools, colleges and universities.

Book Tour

As mentioned, your publisher may not fund a book tour, but that doesn't mean it's out of the question for you. Depending on your budget, you could fund your own regional or national book tour. Your best bet is to start local, and reach out to bookstores, libraries, schools, book clubs, and literary festivals. Ask to be a guest speaker for events specific to your niche or ask to be interviewed for their newsletter. Once you get a yes, schedule your other stops strategically. Be sure to supply promotional materials for the event such as flyers and rack cards, and do your share of promoting as well. This is where LinkedIn and Facebook events will come in handy for your social media marketing efforts.

Virtual Book and Podcast Tours

These days it's become more common to see virtual book tours, as it's easier and more cost-effective to reach the masses online as opposed to traveling to live events and venues. To plan a virtual book tour, start following bloggers, podcasters, and social media pages of influencers in your niche. Compile a list and start to interact in a positive and professional manner. Set a date for your tour and then reach out to everyone on your list individually (you will want to write a personal email for this; no mass emailing here) and ask to be featured on their blog or podcast. Be sure to let them know you are familiar with their work, why you like it, and why you and your book are a good fit for their audience. Your virtual tour may consist of a number of things such as guest blogging, Q&A author interviews, excerpts from your book, podcast or radio appearance, giveaways, webinars, joint ventures, video content, and much more.

Create a Book Funnel

I have many clients who sell their paperbacks through a "free + shipping" book funnel. The idea of this type of book funnel is that you give away a free copy of your paperback (usually on a landing page), but only charge for shipping. Once the prospect enters their credit card information to pay for the shipping, they are redirected to an upsell page or two where the author makes additional offers such as an online course, membership program, one-on-one session, or a mastermind.

Authors usually charge between $7.95 or $9.95 for shipping through these types of book funnels in order to cover their own costs on printing and shipping of the books, so they aren't looking to create income on the front end–these are true authorpreneurs who understand the bulk of their income comes from backend sales.

If you don't want to fuss with printing and shipping, you can always offer a PDF download of your book for a low cost such as $4.95. The goal is to offer your book for a low upfront fee, and then make offers on the backend through upsells.

Think Outside the Box

My mentor and colleague, Sunny Dawn Johnston, wrote *Invoking the Archangels, A Nine-Step Process to Heal Your Body, Mind, and Soul* back in 2011. She was signed by Hierophant Publishing of Hampton Roads, a respectable traditional publisher.

Sunny quickly realized that marketing her book would be due to her own efforts. She knew she had to get creative and think outside the box, because after a traditional publisher takes his cut of your royalties, you are only bringing in about $1 per book. Sunny knew she would have to sell *a lot* of books. So what did she do?

Sunny committed to traveling the country for one full year, at her own expense, and book "living room" book tours. Now, Sunny is well-known in her area of expertise so she had already started building her tribe long before she started writing her book. She used social media and her email list to reach her tribe and announce that she would be traveling the country for a year, on a self-funded book tour to promote her new book, and asked would anyone want her to visit their city. Stipulations were you had to have a minimum of 20 people attend, and there was a cost of $22 per head. I hosted one when Sunny came to Florida and I filled the room with 26 people. Each of them paid me $25 to attend, $22 of which went to Sunny, and I kept the other $3 per person to cover the appetizers and refreshments for the evening and the event venue. (These events weren't always in living rooms, and I hosted my night in a banquet room at a local restaurant.)

Sunny and her soul musician came for three hours, talked about angels and the processes in her book, and built trust within the room. When Sunny was finished, she sold books, workbooks, jewelry, CDs, card decks, and other products at the back of the room. Sunny may only get $1 per book from her publisher when her book is sold online and in bookstores, but she is able to purchase books at wholesale from her publisher at a highly discounted rate and resell at the retail price. She makes more per book through her own efforts than by her web and bookstore sales, from which she makes a royalty, so it was worth it for her to travel the country and do her own self-funded book tour. She was building her tribe, one city at a time, collecting contact info, selling her books for a larger profit, in addition to all the other products she carried along with her.

After traveling the country for a year, Sunny sold 5,000 books on the road and a number of her own supporting products as well. She not only grew her list, but she also got her name and message out to as many people as possible and now has connections all over the country. Now instead of hosting retreats and workshops locally, she has the option to travel all over the country, because she has a following in several cities.

So you see, there are many ways to build your platform and grow your tribe, but one thing is for certain: it won't be by sitting back and waiting for your publisher to fly you around on sightings and signings. You are going to pay out of your own pocket and market your book by your own efforts. And that is why I say the best time to get started building your platform is NOW.

CHAPTER EIGHT

Companion Products For Your Biz

W e've come this far and by now you probably know, your book sales alone are not likely to make you rich. Sure, it happens. There is the book that takes off and spreads like wildfire, ultimately reaching the top of the New York Times bestsellers list, but those are few and far between. The truth is the majority of authors don't make a living from their books alone. You see, it's not your book that makes you the big bucks, although your book is often the most important piece of the puzzle. It's everything you create to offer along with it, the empire you build based on the core concepts of your main message that is more lucrative. The companion products you create, the opportunities that arise, the programs you develop, those all stem from the expertise you share in your book. So writing the book is the first step in building your empire, but it's only one step. Here's where the real money comes in.

Something about writing and publishing a book (when done right) makes you an instant authority in your business. Your book lends you credibility as an expert in your field. It opens doors of opportunity, broadening the stage to reach your tribe and share your message. That's why writing and publishing your book comes first, and everything else evolves from there. Now that you have a book, you can schedule speaking engagements, create companion products, develop mentoring and coaching programs, launch online courses—the high-end items that will be the basis of your business. That's where the income-generating side of authorship is typically made, and that's how you build your empire.

In this chapter, I am going to offer you a variety of options for products and services you can create and incorporate into your own business. Now, please don't feel like you need to add them all, and you certainly don't have to create them all at once, but this will give you ideas, and as your business grows, continue rolling some of that income into a new product or service. And *that's* how empires are built.

Audiobooks

Audiobooks are a nice way you can make additional income off the publication of your book. If you have a publisher, they will likely handle the creation of your eBook and audiobook, but if you've self-published you can also publish your book as an audiobook and make additional income from your already created content. Always be repurposing that content, boys and girls!

Audible, an Amazon company, owns a platform specific to audiobooks: Audiobook Creation Exchange (ACX). So you can almost seamlessly publish your book in audio format and make additional income. Every audiobook you host on ACX will be available on Audible, Amazon, and iTunes, and if you grant

Audible exclusive distribution rights, then you'll earn royalties of 40%. What's convenient about the program is that it caters to the tech savvy or the technically challenged. Once you enroll in the program, in order to create your audiobook, you'll need to either narrate it yourself or allow someone else to narrate it for a percentage of the royalties. If you have a decent voice, the recording equipment or access to a studio, and the time to record and upload your book in sections as required by ACX, then you may consider narrating your own audiobook so you keep the majority of the net royalties.

On the other hand, if you'd like to opt to have a narrator voice the audio for your book, that is an available option directly through the ACX program. Your narrator and you will make a deal, and he or she will either get paid per finished hour or get a portion of the earned royalties, and for some that's a small price to pay to get a book into an audiobook format and make additional income from the content. If your shaking voice or lack of tech-*spertise* is stopping you from creating your audiobook, you are missing out on income. What do you have to lose by allowing a narrator to record the content in exchange for a portion of the royalties you would otherwise not receive if you opted not to add an audiobook?

Not to mention, audiobooks are one of the fastest growing segments of the publishing industry with 71,000 audiobooks published in 2020 with U.S. audiobook revenue reaching $1.3 billion. That's an increase of 39% from 2019, one of the largest upticks of book industry growth within the U.S[3]. I don't know about you, but that's an audience I don't want to miss out on!

---

[3] https://www.zippia.com/advice/us-book-industry-statistics/

TIP: If you decide to create an audiobook, be sure to utilize the $50 Bounty Program. At the time of writing this book, Audible will pay you an additional $50 for each subscriber who signs up for a new account through your affiliate link and downloads your book as their first book with their new subscription.

There are many ways you can publish and distribute your audiobook, but as of 2021 Audible is the most popular audiobook website in the world and reached sales of $940 million, with a growth rate of 24.5%[4]. Audible also has over 200,000 audiobooks available, so that's why ACX.com is my personal choice for audiobook distribution.

Audio Downloads

Digital CDs and MP3s make great companion products, especially if you are a coach or have affirmations or meditations to share. I know many authors with affirmation and meditation CDs, but this is not only for the authors specializing in the spiritual realm. Perhaps you're a health coach and want to record a motivational CD. This can easily be done in many ways, but one way is to go to CD Baby and create an account, upload your audio files, which you've likely created through an audio editing software such as Audacity or Garage Band (both free), and then sell your MP3s as downloads through digital distribution channels such as iTunes, Amazon, Spotify and many more that you can select through the publication process. This way

[4] https://publishingperspectives.com/2021/06/audio-publishers-association-12-percent-audiobook-revenue-growth-in-2020-covid19/

your listeners have the option to download your digital CD tracks separately or they can download the entire CD. If you would like your CD in a physical format, you can use a CD Baby's distribution service or another of your choice, and simply upload your tracks and cover art, and they will manufacture your CDs for a fee.

Companion Journals/Workbooks

Depending on the type of book you write, you may also consider adding a coordinating workbook or journal to bundle along with your book. Why have one book when you can have two, right? Of course, this won't apply to all books, and it's certainly easier to do with a non-fiction book than fiction, but we are talking about creating a book for your business here, so most likely you are writing non-fiction, and your book is probably teaching something of value based on your area of expertise. If so, now you have a chance to develop a second book that should come together quite easily since you already have most of the content created from your principal product, your book. If you introduce concepts in your book, then you could have a separate workbook to help your reader further explore those concepts on a deeper level.

Take my client Darcy Simonson's book, *To Love Your Life*, for example. Darcy is a Life & Spiritual Mentor whose area of expertise is personal growth. She created her book to help her clients live their best life by finding happiness and self-love. Darcy introduces a variety of tools and techniques for her readers in *To Love Your Life*, and throughout her book she mentions the value of using the *To Love Your Life Workbook and Journal*. In the workbook she lists exercises to help you delve deeper in doing the work, and includes questions that prompt you to look within and work through the answers with the journaling space she provides.

This is a great tool for her clients, and she's developed programs based on the book where she also sells it to those who attend her workshops or take her online course. So if someone finds her book, they will see mention of the companion workbook while they are reading. Although the book stands alone as a high-quality product packed with valuable insights (it's 272 pages, after all!), if her readers like her book, her message, her learning style, now they can go to her website and buy the workbook to study her teachings on a deeper level.

But she doesn't stop there. When those readers go to her website she has an opt-in where they can receive her free MP3 download if they sign up for her Weekly Life Letter. Additionally, she posts an online course that will allow them to study even deeper, and if they really resonate with her message they may hire her for one-on-one mentoring and coaching. Can you see how Darcy has built a business with a few add-on programs and companion products? She is the ultimate example of an authorpreneur!

When I wrote *Write from the Heart,* I was at a time in my life when I was working primarily with aspiring authors who wanted to learn how to write a book, and as the Founder of Spiritual Writers Network, I found many of my readers enjoyed spiritual-based techniques to unlock creativity, so in that book I delve into topics such as meditation, visualization, affirmations, and journaling. Since *Write from the Heart* was a workbook in itself, it wouldn't have made sense for me to add an additional companion workbook. So for the companion product I created a simple journal, *Write from the Heart: Writing Prompts, Quotes and*

Inspirations. It's a journal with writing prompts and inspirational quotes sprinkled throughout, but the core of this book is a daily writing journal, so it's mostly filled with journaling lines and space for writing. My target audience at the time loved it, and when I hosted writing retreats it was a popular product on my sales table. When I launched my Write from the Heart 8-Week Book Writing Intensive each year, I would send each student who enrolled in my online course a copy of the journal as a free gift, my way of saying thank you for joining. They loved it! The point here is, don't just stop with one product when you can repurpose the information and develop spin-off books to accompany it.

Card Decks

Depending on what type of book you are writing, card decks or affirmation decks have grown in popularity. Again, this may not work with all genres, but for some, card decks make great companion products. I'll give you a few examples.

I have a client who wrote a book on animal communication, so she developed a card deck with an animal on each and a message on the back. I have another client who writes books about angels, so she created a deck of Angel cards to accompany the book. Another of my clients wrote a book about losing her son, and she created a card deck so that grieving mothers could receive messages from Spirit. Each card has an uplifting message, and the cards are so beautiful it's hard not to purchase the bundle when you buy the book! And when I wrote *Write from the Heart,* I created an affirmation deck for writers. Do you see where this is going? It's just one more example of a physical product you can create for back-of-the-room sales at events and on your website.

Online Courses

This is one product that can bring in a good chunk of income, so don't skip this section. If your book is non-fiction and teaches something of value, it's pretty easy to break the chapters into sections and create an online course by offering a deeper dive into the content. And, depending on whether your course is live or evergreen, offering additional support.

Online courses are delivered in a variety of styles, and a good online course will have lessons in a variety of mediums to appeal to all learning styles. Some of your prospective audience will learn better visually while others prefer audio. I personally like to print worksheets that I can sit down and read, so PDF downloads are my preferred learning style. If you create an online course, keep in mind that you will have a variety of students. So your course content should be delivered in a variety of ways, including audio, video, screen share, text files, and PDF downloads. Sounds like a ton of work, right? I'm here to tell you, it's well worth the time and effort. Online courses are my preferred companion product, and I'll tell you why.

Once you write your book, the foundational content is already created. Now, of course, you will expand upon the information in your book and add additional content, or else why would anyone join your course when they could just buy your book, right? But the foundation of your course will already be created from your book, and then you can add additional content, bonus materials, video tutorials, audio, Zoom sessions, closed Facebook groups for support, and access to *you* on a more personal level. For your tribe, that's priceless, and once you offer access to yourself through an online course, you will establish trust within your tribe. If you develop a high-quality course and make yourself available when the course is live, you will create long-term relationships with your students, who will then go on to buy your other products, attend your events and look to you as their mentor, signing up for your high-end coaching offers or done-for-you services. And that, my friends, is your empire.

Here's some simple course math you can use to gauge how much you could potentially make on the launch of an online course (or any product you are launching), in relation to the size of your list. Follow this simple formula:

List x **$ of Program** x **.03** (3% conversion rate) = **Launch $**

Example:

Sally has a warm list of 1,000 subscribers. Her online course is $497. On average, she should be able to convert at least 3% of her list (granted they are a targeted and engaged list) during her product launch.

1,000 (list) x **497** (price of product) x **.03** (3%) = **$14,910**

Do you see how online courses can be lucrative?

Before I moved my courses to ClickFunnels, I housed them on Teachable. One thing I liked about Teachable is that they were always developing training for the instructors who house their schools and courses on their platform. The course math mentioned above was something I learned through a course they created called The Profitable Teacher. When I learned this formula I had already been running my online courses for nearly two years. I went back through my launch numbers and applied the formula to see how accurate it is, and to my delight, it's spot-on, give or take a percentage point or two. Some products convert better than others, so 3% is a good average, and for me that's low-balling it. Now I know I can use this formula each time I price out a new product to get an idea of how much I will bring in during its launch based on the size of my list.

As mentioned, you're going to want a warm and engaged list for this, so it's a good idea to incorporate some list-building activities into the frontend of your launch such as a free 5-day challenge, masterclass or video series, and then open enrollment for your course at the end.

Evergreen vs. Live

If you decide to launch an online course, you must first decide if you want an evergreen option, meaning your students can enroll anytime, or you will do a live launch, where you have a dedicated launch at certain points throughout the year, making the course only available during that time and everyone starts the course together on the same day. Both have their pros and cons. I offer both types of courses, so I'll offer feedback from my experiences with each.

After I wrote *Write from the Heart*, I decided to create an online course based on that book, and thus the 8-Week Book Writing Intensive was born. This was a live course that I launched once per year, and each time I typically ended up with approximately 18-20 participants. I actually had to cap enrollment at 20 due to the engagement I offered during the live course. My students knew what date the course would start, and we all worked through the eight weeks together. Every Monday at 9 am, a new module of content would become available. The modules consisted of a video, audio, PDF workbook and a few worksheets to help them further develop their ideas. If they had questions along the way, I encouraged them to post their questions in our private Facebook group so everyone could benefit from the info. In addition to the course content, I offered two live Q&A calls at week four and week eight, where they could ask questions about the materials covered thus far.

At the end of each 8-week session, everyone had grown closer and the Facebook group became a valuable asset where they could share and find support in a safe place. Plus they felt as if they belonged to a community, and they loved that! After the course, many of my students became my coaching clients, and I went on to help publish their books; they also attended my writing retreats and live events.

This is just one example of how you can create a course, or high-end program, based on your book. At the time, it was my flagship program so it was important for me to run it live so I could add some high value components such as access to me in the Facebook group, the live calls, and written feedback on their opening chapter.

I also have several other smaller courses that are evergreen, or on-demand, meaning they are available for enrollment anytime, and the students gain access to all the content upon registration and are free to work at their own pace. I don't offer one-on-one access to me through live calls, email or a Facebook group, so these courses usually have a lower price point than a live course.

As you can see there is more time and energy invested with a live course, and it's easier to funnel students in with a live launch phase, because you set aside a time frame of anywhere between two to six weeks for concentrated efforts of promoting the course through early-bird rates that entice them because they can get a discount, and then many buy last minute when you announce the space is nearly full or the cart is closing. Having said that, there may be less time and energy involved when students are taking an evergreen course since they have access to the content upfront and work at their own pace. But it takes a constant effort to drive traffic to those courses since you likely will not have dedicated launch phases throughout the year, although you could. You'll have to get creative with an evergreen course and consistently work on growing your list, and driving traffic to the course through YouTube, auto-webinars, social media, and advertising.

> **TIP:** If you create an evergreen course, consider offering your readers a discount code for enrollment at the back of your book. Now you have your call-to-action and this offers your readers an incentive to join your course since they are getting a discount on enrollment.

TO Self-host or NOT to Self-host

Once you decide whether you want your course live or evergreen, you will need to find a platform from which to deliver the content. This is where you have options.

> **Self-hosting:** If you self-host your course, you will need to add the content to a website that you own and pay for web hosting. You will likely need a plugin for the membership site software, and you'll need to be somewhat tech savvy to design the membership site or else have the funds to hire someone to design it for you. In either case, you'll need a decent knowledge of how the backend of your site works in order to manage your students, payments, and list integration.

Dedicated platform: For this option, you would host your course(s) on a dedicated platform such as Click-Funnels, Teachable, or Kajabi—there are many to choose from, so do your research, but those are three I've used myself and know enough about to recommend. You will pay a fee to host your courses there (usually monthly with discounts if you select the annual plan) and they will handle the payments through a Strip and/or PayPal integration. With self-hosting you have to integrate your shopping cart with your website and set up payment options, and that's not always easy. If you are looking for ease of use, one of these dedicated platforms may be right for you. Many even offer a built-in affiliate program so your students can promote and share your course in exchange for a commission, offering you additional exposure for your course.

I started off self-hosting and spent a ton of money learning how to create a course on my own site, as well as adding costly plugins for my membership site and affiliate program. I integrated my mailing list with my WishList Member plugin, and used PayPal for payment processing, but still had to create PayPal buttons for installment plans to offer my students a variety of payment options on the sales page I also had to create and install. If you use PayPal you must upgrade to a business account in order to offer subscription and installment plans; otherwise, you will find you are sending out invoices each month and chasing money from your students.

Mid-way into my third time running the 8-Week Book Writing Intensive, my site was hacked and my students were unable to login. Luckily I had been thinking about moving my courses over to Teachable for some time, so I could create my own branded school and house all my courses on one platform. This emergency situation prompted me to go ahead and move my course over, and within two hours I had everything loaded up for my new school— videos, audios, PDF's, worksheets, etc. My students reported liking the new platform much better, because all the content was contained in one area, divided by sections, with lectures added to each that they could easily navigate. And since my students had already paid for the course, I was able to create a coupon code so they could access the course on the new platform for free.

I now use ClickFunnels and couldn't be happier with it. Since I do a lot of marketing for my courses leading up to a launch through free challenges, webinars, and lead magnets, ClickFunnels makes it easy to create all of those things in one place, on one platform. Everything I need is available through their platform such as opt-in forms, sales pages, order forms, payment integration, email marketing, and membership areas to house my courses–this makes online marketing a breeze, and honestly, my conversion rates have increased dramatically since switching over.

There are also course marketplaces such as Udemy or SkillShare, where you can add your courses to their platform, and as an added bonus, they have members and students of their own, so you don't need to be constantly driving traffic to make sales there. Udemy currently has 46 million students, but they also have over 175,000 online courses in their marketplace[5], so

---

[5] https://en.wikipedia.org/wiki/Udemy#:~:text=It%20was%20founded%20 in%20May,courses%20in%20over%2075%20languages.

without some marketing efforts on your behalf, your courses can get lost in the sea of the online courses they offer.

Udemy caps the price you can charge for your course, so this is a nice place to repurpose your low-end evergreen courses once they are created and launched through another platform, as an additional way to make some passive income from your content, but it's not a place for your high-end courses. Udemy is also not a place to get rich, per se, although some are finding great success. I've found those success stories from Udemy come from very concentrated marketing efforts from instructors with multiple courses on their platform. I gave Udemy a good year of my life before removing my courses from sale. The downside to Udemy, besides the price cap, is that you don't get access to your students' email addresses and it is against policy to direct them off the platform and onto your mailing list.

Membership Programs

Another popular way to create some passive monthly income in your business is to create a membership program. This is where your members will usually pay for a monthly membership, with discounts at the annual level, and where their membership grants them access into a password-protected site containing valuable content, which is usually accompanied by a private Facebook group. The allure of a membership site for the authorpreneur is, of course, the passive monthly income.

Depending on your book or business topic, your membership site could be your flagship product. For example, a health coach may have a membership site where members can access tutorial videos, recipes, a community of like-minded co-members, and an A-Z listing of ailments and recommended natural remedies, with resource.

If you are going to have a membership site, be sure to add valuable content and update it often to keep it relevant. You'll want to always be adding new content so your members have a reason to keep their membership active, and consider offering support to your members through monthly training, Q&A, and Zoom sessions. The motto, under promise and over deliver, applies here as well.

Coaching and Mentoring Programs

One of the best upsells you can make, in my opinion, is a coaching or mentoring program. You are the expert in your area of expertise ... you just wrote an entire book on it, after all! If you've created a high-quality book and you've delivered valuable information that can help others, those who were moved or touched by your work will become your tribe, and would most likely *love* to work one-on-one with you.

This option is not for everyone, and some would rather only develop online courses and membership programs to be able to serve more people and to make that income without having to work one-on-one with their clients, but others thrive on the personal interaction, and for them, this is ideal.

I personally enjoy working one-on-one with my clients because it brings me pleasure to help them realize their goals and take them from having a general book idea to becoming a best-selling author. I like to read their stories and get to know them, and it brings me great satisfaction to watch them evolve throughout the process of working together and to know I've made a difference in their lives. However, due to the level of attention and time that's involved, I can only take on so many private clients each year, so working one-on-one with me involves a premium investment, and it will likely be the same for you once you grow and scale your empire.

There may come a time when you are so busy you can't take on those one-on-one clients, and if you do, your rate will likely be high-end. As our businesses grow and our time becomes scarcer, we are often forced to raise our prices. What's interesting is when you begin pricing your services higher it brings value to you and your business and you'll find that you tend to attract clients who are more driven and easier to work with at the high-end level. Often, the more they've invested in your program, the more seriously they will take it. Keep this in mind when pricing your mentoring and coaching services. You may start off on the lower end, but as your business grows you may find it's better to have a few high-end clients to work with than dozens of low-end clients who are not taking you or your time seriously.

I'm a firm believer in everyone having a mentor, especially if you want to move forward in your business. I'm not only a mentor myself, but I realize that I am also a work-in-progress and I need to be evolving in life and in business. I've paid as much as $35,000 per year to work with one of my business coaches. A good mentor can help you take great strides forward that may have otherwise taken you years on your own. I look at mentoring as an investment in my business—a fastpass to success. Plus, you can learn from your teachers, and pass that information along to your students. Every successful person I know has a mentor, and if your tribe is serious about their growth, they will see the value in having a mentor, too.

You may be wondering how to even begin a mentoring program. There are many ways you can do this. One way is to simply announce that you are opening a limited number of spaces in your schedule to work one-on-one with a few select clients, and due to time constraints, you can only take a certain number of people (be mindful not to take on more than you can handle). You might even ask them to apply to participate in your program and have them fill out an online application or have a Zoom or phone interview with you. This is ideal, because if you can get them on a call, you have a better chance of answering their questions and helping them to make the decision to work with you.

Another way to do this is to offer it as an upgrade to your online course. So when your students register, they are then redirected to an upsell page where they are asked if they would like to add on one-on-one coaching or enter your mentoring program. Of course, there will be an additional fee, and it will likely be substantial. They are getting personalized access to you, after all.

I personally wouldn't offer a high-end upsell on the front-tend, when a student enrolls. I usually offer it when the program is ending, after the student has gotten to know me better. For example, at the end of my current flagship program, the Author Success Academy, I offer my students an opportunity to use a portion of their enrollment as a credit toward my Deluxe Best-selling Author Package, where I work one-on-one with them as their personal project manager to take them from manuscript to bestselling author.

My business has grown by leaps and bounds, so I view mentoring as an investment not only in my business, but also myself. If you want to grow a profitable business based on the concepts of your book, consider becoming a mentor or coach in your area of expertise. This will allow you to have clients all across the globe who you connect with online, by phone, or Zoom.

Masterminds

Once you become respected and well-known in your field, you can even head a high-end mastermind program. This is where you will meet with your mentoring clients weekly or monthly over a longer period of time, in an intimate group setting.

For instance, I participated in a high-end 12-month mastermind with a business mentor and 19 other members. Over the course of 12 months, we had a two-day live mastermind event in a tropical location, bi-weekly calls, a membership site to access our modules and training materials, and six emergency sessions to use via phone or Zoom with our mentor as needed. It was a steep investment, but a small price to pay to learn from her expertise and follow in the footsteps of those who have done it, made mistakes, and can tell you what to do and what not to do. Not to mention, I learned a lot from the other members as they navigated success in their own businesses and offered valuable feedback and support to me as well.

In-Person Workshops/Retreats

Workshops and retreats are a great way to get your clients together for a day or weekend gathering and really dive in to the teachings in your book. Plus, if you have a companion workbook that accompanies your book, you can make it required material for the event, or you can include a copy with their registration. This is also a good way to sell your books and other companion products via back-of-the-room sales. Have a table set up to display your books, journals, card decks, and any other products you may have to offer. At the end of the event this is a good time to make an offer exclusive to attendees. Be sure to put a time limit on the offer to encourage enrollment. This could be anything from one-on-one coaching or a mentoring program, to an online course you are launching, to enrollment into your prestigious mastermind. Hosting events are a great way to connect with your tribe, get to know them, establish trust and promote your other products and services.

Virtual Workshops

Virtual Workshops are an easy way to bring in some additional income without having to get too technical as most can be done right on Zoom. For example, you could host a two-day virtual retreat, four-week group coaching program, or perhaps a one-day workshop. You could even host a series of monthly Zoom classes, choosing a subtopic for each month.

When the globally pandemic hit in 2020 and shut down businesses and travel, I was forced to cancel my writing retreat scheduled to take place in the Florida Keys. However, I still wanted to offer writing support to my attendees who had registered and anyone else who was looking to write a book that would like to join us. My co-facilitator and I decided to host a virtual writing retreat instead, all on Zoom, with a private Facebook group for the attendees to connect. We all met virtually for a Friday evening meet-and-greet, followed by two full-day workshops, on Saturday and Sunday. We were even able to put small groups into breakout rooms via Zoom for various exercises, and since there wasn't as much overhead as an in-person retreat would require, it turned out to be quite lucrative.

Technology allows us to connect with our clients and students all over the world. There's no better time to embrace the online world and carve out a place in your niche.

Affiliate and Referral Programs

Once you set up all these programs, the greatest difficulty you will encounter is getting new clients to find your products and services in the first place. That is sometimes the hardest part, and this is where having a strong list will come into play. One other option is to get your current clients and colleagues who believe in you and your work to promote your products and services for you in exchange for a commission. This is often done through an affiliate or referral program.

There are affiliate plugins you can install right into your WordPress website, and as discussed earlier, many platforms such as ClickFunnels, Teachable and Kajabi have built-in affiliate programs for your online courses and membership sites. No matter what platform or plugin you choose, be sure to have software to manage this for you. The software will create custom links with your affiliate's custom tractable ID embedded, so when your affiliate shares your program or service and someone signs up after clicking that link (tracked with cookies), the affiliate gets credit for the sale, and can often access their reports right from the affiliate center. Many affiliate systems will manage the payouts as well, so it can virtually run while you are sleeping, and that's ideal.

If you have happy clients or students who believe in your message and what you have to offer, consider asking them to be an affiliate for you, especially if they have a large list of their own. What better way to expand your reach! And people tend to make decisions based on referrals and word of mouth more often than not. Having your clients and students endorse you and your business is the ultimate compliment.

Through Transcendent Publishing, we offer a referral program and we let our authors know that in their exit email, after we've published and launched their book. For every client they refer to us, we offer a percentage of the package price back to the person who referred them. Because of this, along with offering great service, of course, we don't have to invest in advertising because we have a constant stream of referrals coming in from our past clients. Therefore, we are happy to pay out the referral fee because it keeps our publishing queue filled.

These are just a few of the examples of how you can create additional products and programs to complement your business, with your book as the foundation of it all. Don't stop when your book is published; that is just the beginning! With each new burst of success, reinvest and create a new product, begin a new class, upgrade your level of coaching. Before long, you will find that you have built your empire.

CHAPTER NINE

Creating More Books & Marketing Within Your Book

Once you have one book under your belt, before long, you'll want to create another, and another, and hopefully, you will take action on your ideas when you get such hunches. Pay attention to what comes up; you are a creative person, and the more you tap into your power, the more ideas will come. You may even want to keep a notepad with you or use an app on your phone to jot down your inspirations. Don't delete them or discredit them, you never know when those ideas will come in handy.

Always be listening to the needs of your readers, students, clients—your tribe. Their needs are your demand, and it's your job to supply that demand. I often come up with my next course or book idea by listening to what my clients and students are asking for, paying attention to the questions I am asked over and over, and even sending out a survey to my mailing list from time to time to see what my tribe needs and wants.

That's how this book idea came to be. During one of my book-writing courses, I started noticing a pattern. When we would come to the module where I would begin to talk about building an author platform, many of my students would freeze up or skip it altogether. They would tell me they were not tech savvy, didn't know where to begin, or just didn't know how to tie it all together. Since that course is primarily on how to write a book, I only spend one module on platform-building, and as you can see from the contents in this book, I couldn't possibly cover it all in one module/week. That's when I knew I needed to create a new sector to my offerings. I would create a book on platform-building, and eventually turn it into another course. But as I was planning, I started to pay attention to what others were asking from me. I was starting to get calls from my colleagues, asking me about online marketing. I would get requests from clients who would ask me to help them get a shopping cart set up on their website so they could sell their books. I was called to be a speaker at business conferences as an author coach, and asked to teach on how to create a book for a business.

Do you see what was happening? I was being called to write *this* book, and if I hadn't listened to what those around me were asking for, I may have missed it and this book would've never come into existence, nor would have the many online programs that came to be after its first edition was published. Always be listening to what your students, clients and colleagues are asking you about, asking you for, and what information you find that you are repeating often. Those are great indications of your next book idea or program, but it's up to you to act on those needs and supply what people need.

As you are writing one book, you will likely get an idea for another book. Don't push it to the back of your mind because you don't want to get distracted from the task at hand. Jot it down in your black book of ideas, and keep them (never delete!); you never know when that idea will come to fruition. Go through your list often when you feel the urge to develop a new product or service. Don't discount those intuitive nudges you get along the way. Your higher self will not lead you astray.

Creating a Series of Books

I've said it before and I'll say it again, you're probably not going to retire on your book sales, although it does happen for some. Typically, it's everything that comes in addition to the book, your backend offers, that earn you the most income. However, if you can come up with a series of books that piggyback off each other, you will have the opportunity to sell more books, and more books means more profits for your business.

Let's take this book as an example. This book is packed with a ton of ideas and concepts you can incorporate into your business. I couldn't possibly break down the creation process for each concept, because this book would end up reading more like a textbook, and who wants to read a textbook? What I could do is break down each section and make it its own book in the *Savvy Authorpreneur* series (hold please, while I write this idea down!). For example, I could have a book on platform-building, another on list building, one on creating a funnel, another dedicated to creating companion products—each could easily stand alone. Each book would be part of the series, and at the back of the book I would list the other books in the series. In the digital edition I would add a hyper-link to the other books in the series, so when the reader was done with one book they could simply click on the next book, buy it and keep reading.

This is easy to do with eBooks, and it's not uncommon to see shorter eBooks of approximately 25,000 words, so I could potentially set out to write four 25,000-word eBooks based on the main topics inside this book yet delve much deeper into each concept, call it the *Savvy Authorpreneur* series, and in the back of each book, link to the next book to encourage more sales. You have to love Amazon for their one-click-buy feature. It makes buying eBooks a breeze for the reader, and it's a beautiful thing for those of us with a series, collecting royalty payments each month.

Not to mention, now I'd have four different eBooks out there attracting readers into my world, where they'd learn about my other products and services, get invited into my community, join my mailing list, and potentially, one day, become clients.

If I were going to create a series of eBooks based on this book and call it the *Savvy Authorpreneur* series, I would price the first book in the series lower than the rest, probably at .99 cents. *What?!* You are probably thinking: Why would I spend all that time and energy creating a book and then price it for .99 cents? Because my goal with the first book is not to make money from that particular book. The goal of the first book in a series is to funnel readers into the series, and avid eBook readers love .99 cent books. Plus, if your first book in the series is .99 cents, you can always be running .99-cent promotions with book promotion companies. This is not only a great strategy to get readers filtered into your book series, but also to rank your book higher on Amazon, resulting in more sales. A .99-cent book will get more downloads, and downloads will raise your ranking on Amazon, often pushing you to the top of your category on the bestsellers list. You could host a paid promotion once per month to keep filtering readers into your series, and once they start reading they are going to want the next book in the series as soon as they finish the last, which will be listed at a higher price.

This doesn't have to be accomplished only with eBooks either, you could create a series of print books in your area of expertise, and this usually happens by default when your first book does well; you start wondering what you could create as a spinoff of the first.

Take author Timothy Ferriss, for example. His book, *The 4-Hour Work Week*, quickly became a #1 New York Times Bestseller. Being the savvy authorpreneur that Mr. Ferriss is, he saw an opportunity to keep that momentum going. He now has *The 4-Hour Body*, *The 4-Hour Chef*, and *The 4-Hour Work Week Expanded Edition*. Not only does he have all these additional books, he has a blog, a podcast, and a TV show! Ferriss was a great inspiration to me many years ago when I read the first edition of *The 4-Hour Work Week* back in 2007. If you haven't read that book, I highly recommend adding the updated and expanded edition to your "to-read" list. Your entrepreneurial spirit will thank you.

List Building Within Your Book

Unfortunately Amazon, Barnes and Noble, and other book retailers don't give you the contact information of your readers, so you never really know who is buying and reading your book, outside of your own concentrated sales efforts. What a shame! How then can we reach our devoted fans when we release our next book, product or service? This is precisely why you need to get your readers to join your mailing list.

A concept that is growing in popularity, one you almost never see a book published without nowadays, is the free bonus gift/ lead magnet with an opt-in to link the reader to the author's list.

Somewhere in your book you'll want to drive traffic to an opt-in form, where you will offer your reader an awesome free bonus, something of value in exchange for their email address, therefore adding your reader to your mailing list.

As a book coach, I'm always encouraging my authors to add a bonus inside their books as a way to capture the reader's interest, and their contact information. Think about it. This person spent a decent amount of time invested in your book, and if they like it, they would more than likely buy your next book, or your online course that accompanies the book, or join your mentoring or mastermind program. But how will they ever know about the additional products you create after the book is published if you don't get them on your list? Someone who has invested time and money into your book, and enjoys your writing and teaching style, is far more likely to work with you and buy your other products. They are your tribe! You *must* capture that information.

In the interest of being transparent, I'm going to go out and say it: I want you on my list. So I am going to offer you a freebie and ask you to go grab it on my website under the "freebies" section: www.shandatrofe.com.

And when you get there you'll be asked to enter your name and email address in exchange for your freebie. But I'm giving you my free report: **My Top 20 Tools for Building an Author Empire** (which you've seen me mention a few times throughout the book).

You've made it this far with me, so hopefully you have some interest in what I have to offer. Maybe not. If not, that's fine too. Not everyone will want to be on your list. But for those who do, offer them a way to continue to work with you!

Do you see how easy that is? A lead magnet for your book can be anything from a free report, a checklist, an MP3, to a PDF workbook that your reader can download. Just be sure it is something of value. If you are always offering valuable free content, and over-delivering on your promises, that is a sure-fire way to build a loyal following and grow your community.

Call-to-Action Page

At the back of your book, you'll want to add a strong call-to-action page. This is usually one of the final pages a reader will come to, and it will offer your reader an opportunity to continue the journey with you, usually on a deeper level than the book can offer. To get an idea of what I'm talking about, notice when you get to the back of this book how I share my other offers with you. You may be thinking this is a bit overzealous. Why? The whole reason for this book is to teach you how to build an empire based on your book, to repurpose your content and create additional companion products based on your book. So why wouldn't I, at the very end, have a strong call-to-action page inviting you to join my Facebook group, promoting my flagship program, or inviting you to work one-on-one with me?

Think about it, if someone doesn't like my book, if the message doesn't resonate with him, or he just doesn't like me as an author, he will put this book down long before he ever finds that call-to-action page. But for the reader who couldn't put the book down, the one who invested their time and energy reading every last word, taking it all in because they too want to build their empire, that's who I want to reach on my call-to-action page, because that is the type of person I want as a client. That's the type of person I want to mentor. That's who I want in my masterminds and at my events. That's who I want to help publish and launch their book to the world.

What if someone finished reading and wanted more, but didn't have a way to connect with me or know where to find me? Or perhaps they didn't know that I have offers at various levels, or that I was open to working with them at all. Then I would have missed out on a huge opportunity to embrace a new client or student, and in that case, shame on me.

Not everyone who reads your book will want to opt in to your list, read your future books, take your courses, or join your tribe, and that's OK. Your book should offer incredible value and stand on its own for your reader. But for the handful (and hopefully more!) who do, be sure you have your contact information, an opt-in for your mailing list, a strong call-to-action, and a way for them to connect with you once having read the book.

Don't skip this step. Those who make it to the last page of your book are usually (not always, but usually) your tribe. Make them an offer and tell them how they can continue to work with you.

CHAPTER TEN

Conclusion: Tying it All Together

Throughout this book I've shown you a variety of tools and techniques to implement to create and grow your empire, but you may be feeling overwhelmed, wondering where to start and how to apply it to your business. I've created a simple acronym to help you develop a clear plan of action to build and grow your empire.

E – Explore your passions and gifts and discover your purpose. Find your target audience and create your unique brand.

M- Manuscript. Write and publish a high-quality book in your area of expertise. This is the foundation of your empire, so be sure to offer your value to your readers.

P- Platform. Build a solid author platform to find your tribe, grow your list, promote your brand, and create your online presence.

I – Implement. Listen to your community and develop content, products and services based on their demand.

R- Repurpose. Create companion products and programs based on the core concepts introduced in your book to offer a deeper dive into the content. Create backend offers and offer additional support for your readers who want more of what you have to offer.

E –Execute your plan. Create a deadline for completing your book, choose a publishing option, build your platform, grow your list, add a new companion product each time you make profits, and always be driving traffic to your products and services!

If you follow these steps you will build a solid business with your book at the foundation of it all. Remember to take it one step at a time, and don't overextend yourself. Time management will be a key influencer when building your empire; you're building a business, after all, and that takes time, dedication, and discipline. Successful entrepreneurs are excellent with time management, and are self-starters with impeccable discipline. You can't give up when the going gets tough, and you can't get lazy with the creation of your book, products and service. And you must always, always be driving traffic to your mailing list and funnel, and that takes a concentrated effort on your behalf. I never said it would be easy, but I promise you it will be worth it if you keep moving forward and take it one step at a time.

> **Success is the sum of small efforts—repeated day in and day out.**
>
> **—Robert Collier**

Now that you are almost finished reading this book and you are ready to build your empire, make a commitment to a minimum of three years to build and grow your business, but don't stop there. Make the commitment to yourself that no matter what, even when the going gets tough, you are not going to give up. You may have to keep your day job for a while as you build your empire; this isn't a get-rich-quick scheme, but this is building a lucrative business that will become your life's work, and that will prove to be exhausting from time to time. However, you can't give up. If you don't want it badly enough, you will let it go. But if it's your passion, and you have a desire to share your gifts and message with the world, I'm a firm believer that when we follow our bliss the universe aligns us with opportunity. Get off track and you will encounter obstacles. Now, that's not saying you won't have a few obstacles while building your business; that's inevitable, as that's how we grow and learn. But if you are truly in alignment with your passions and your purpose, the universe will reward you with opportunity and abundance, if you allow it.

The Journey Continues

Throughout this book I've shared about the importance of your call-to-action page. Well, here is mine. Not everyone, but most people that get to the back of your book, may be interested in working with you further or at least joining your mailing list, community, and consuming additional content. If that's you, I want to offer you a variety of options, from my free Facebook group or masterclass to my flagship program or done-for-you service.

Self-Publishing Success Facebook Group: This is a free community where I post valuable self-publishing and book marketing strategies. It's a great place to seek support and connect with other authors on a similar journey as you. Join us: www.facebook.com/groups/selfpublishingsuccessgroup

The Author Success Academy: This is my flagship program which comes with seven modules of content designed to help you write your bestseller, build your author platform, and publish and launch your book like a pro. As a member, you'll receive group coaching from me, along with lifetime access to our private Facebook community and modules, so you can gain support as needed yet work at your own pace through the program's content. Visit: www.workwithshanda.com

Deluxe Bestselling Author Program: Due to high demand, space for my done-for-you service is limited, as I can only partner with a small number of one-on-one clients per year. Please be advised that this is a premium offer for the aspiring author who doesn't wish to learn all the ins and outs of self-publishing, and instead desires to work closely with me and my team of design professionals at Transcendent Publishing to create your high-quality book and launch it to the world. I have a 64-point system to take my clients from manuscript to Amazon #1 bestselling author, and I walk you through the entire process as your personal project manager and coach. If you're interested in working one-on-one with me through my *Deluxe Bestselling Author Package* (typically 3-6 months), please apply here: www.workwithshanda.com.

To your success,
Shanda Trofe

About the Author

As the founder of Transcendent Publishing, Shanda Trofe has been helping authors reach their writing and publishing goals since 2012. She specializes in teaching book-writing, publishing, and marketing strategies for coaches, healers, speakers and entrepreneurs.

Shanda's passion lies in helping authors turn their message into their life's work by creating viable businesses through authorship, and she enjoys working with her clients throughout the entire process, from idea to publication. To date, Shanda has launched over 500 #1 bestselling books for her clients, and has worked with thousands of students through her online courses and coaching programs

Shanda resides in Saint Petersburg, Florida with her husband and their adored fur babies.

CONTACT:

Email:
info@shandatrofe.com

Website:
www.shandatrofe.com
www.transcendentpublishing.com

Facebook:
www.facebook.com/shandatrofe
www.facebook.com/transcendentpublishing

Instagram:
www.instagram.com/shandatrofe
www.instagram.com/transcendent_publishing